HAIL
MARY

HAIL MARY

A Marian Book of Hours

compiled by

William G. Storey, D.M.S.

Professor Emeritus of Liturgy
University of Notre Dame

ave maria press   Notre Dame, Indiana

Unless otherwise noted, scripture passages and canticles used in this book are taken from the *New Revised Standard Version* of the Bible, copyright © 1993 and 1989 by the Division of Christian Education of the National Council of Churches of Christ in the U.S.A. Used by permission. All rights reserved.

Selected Psalms are taken from *The Psalms: Grail Translation from the Hebrew*, copyright © 1993 by The Grail, England. Used by permission of A.P. Watt, Ltd. on behalf of the Grail, England. All rights reserved.

Further acknowledgments are found on pp. 313-316.

© 2002 by Ave Maria Press, Inc.

Founded in 1865, Ave Maria Press is a ministry of the Indiana Province of Holy Cross.

Founded in 1865, Ave Maria Press is a ministry of the Indiana Province of Holy Cross.

www.avemariapress.com

ISBN-10 1-59471-104-6   ISBN-13 978-1-59471-104-6

Cover and text design by Katherine Robinson Coleman

Interior photos by Artville, Corbis and Photodisc

Printed and bound in the United States of America.

Library of Congress Cataloging-in-Publication Data

Hail Mary : a Marian book of hours / compiled, arranged and translated by William G. Storey.

       p. cm.

ISBN-13: 978-1-59471-104-6 (pbk.)

ISBN-10: 1-59471-104-6 (pbk.)

1. Mary, Blessed Virgin, Saint--Prayer-books and devotions--English.
2. Catholic Church--Prayer-books and devotions--English. 3. Devotional calendars--Catholic Church. I. Storey, William George, 1923-BX2160.23 .H35 2002

242'.802--dc21

2001005603

CIP

Contents

$\mathcal{I}$NTRODUCTION

There is no doubt that whatever we say
in praise of the Mother touches the Son,
and when we honor the Son
we detract nothing from the Mother's glory.

St. Bernard of Clairvaux (1090–1153)[1]

Although we live in what has often been called the Age of Mary, Marian devotions have suffered an exceptional decline in many places today. One of the ironies of our current situation is that those who love Mary are—for the first time in a thousand years—largely deprived of a Marian Office. There are various good reasons for this, with the appearance of the new Liturgy of the Hours in the years after the Second Vatican Council being the most notable.

But perhaps it is now time to reinvigorate what was a mainstay of Christian prayer and Marian devotion for much of the church's history, the Marian Office. This book aims to provide such an office, one that will be fully orthodox, reasonably brief and simple, and in line with the reform thrust of the Second Vatican Council. But before we look at the structure and the parts of such an office, let us review its history and theology.

History and Theology of the Marian Office

The oldest surviving prayer to the Virgin Mary was discovered in Egypt in 1917 and contains the second oldest reference to Mary as *Theotokos* (Greek: God-bearer; Latin: *Deipara, Dei Genetrix*; English: Mother of God). Here is a modern English version:

We turn to you for protection,
holy Mother of God (*Theotokos*).
Listen to our prayers
and help us in our needs.
Save us from every danger,
glorious and blessed Virgin.[2]

This remarkable prayer of the late second or early third century first appeared in Coptic and Greek, probably in the great Church of Alexandria. In one form or another it soon entered the liturgies of East and West and has been enshrined there ever since.

When the ancient title *Theotokos* became a bone of contention in the early fifth century, the third Ecumenical Council (Ephesus, 431) vindicated it against theologians and bishops who preferred to call her only Mother of Christ. The Council of Ephesus ratified *Theotokos* as a perfectly adequate and correct expression of the church's immemorial faith in the Incarnate Word and of Mary's role in our salvation.

One of the first results of this definition was an explosion of popular joy and unparalleled devotion to "the great Mother of God, Mary most holy." It took the form of sermons of exultation and congratulation, new feasts, liturgies, hymns, prayers, icons, churches, shrines, and pilgrimages. In Constantinople alone, the devout Empress Pulcheria (399–453) erected three magnificent churches in honor of Mary *Theotokos*: Blachernai, containing the Virgin's shroud; Hodegoi, with its famous icon of "Mary the Guide," thought to have been painted by St. Luke himself; and Chalkoprateia, which enshrined the Virgin's cincture.

Such fervent Marian devotion was epitomized in the Byzantine *Akathistos* Hymn, or "Exaltation of the Mother of God," a song of ecstatic praise composed in the fifth century for the feast of the Annunciation (March 25). It became *the* popular devotion among the Orthodox and soon entered the liturgy of Constantinople and its many daughter churches. "The *Akathistos* is the most beautiful, the most profound, the most ancient Marian hymn in all Christian literature."[3]

Exaltation of the Mother of God

While we sing to your divine Child,
O great Mother of God,
we praise you as his living temple.
The Lord who upholds the universe
came to dwell in your womb
and sanctified and glorified you
and taught everyone to cry out to you:
Rejoice, tabernacle of the Word of God!
Rejoice, holiest of all the saints!
Rejoice, golden ark of the covenant!
Rejoice, treasury of divine life!
Rejoice, precious diadem of Christian rulers!
Rejoice, pride and joy of devout priests!
Rejoice, impregnable rampart of the Church!
Rejoice, invincible wall of the kingdom of God!
Rejoice, giver of victory over evil!
Rejoice, destroyer of all who attack us!
Rejoice, healing of minds and bodies!
Rejoice, salvation of souls!
Rejoice, unwedded Bride!

Byzantine Akathist Hymn, eikos 12

The Latin Churches of the West were a bit slower than the Greek and Syriac East in developing their Marian piety and devotions. By the late sixth century, however, they began to establish a series of Christological and Marian feasts—largely modeled on those of the East—that expressed and fostered a deep Marian piety. One small but influential part of this development was the introduction of the *Sub tuum praesidium* into the Roman liturgy by the Syrian Pope Sergius I (687–701) for the feast of Mary's Assumption (August 15).

Such developments were only the beginning of a long devotional evolution. In the ninth century monks and nuns began to celebrate a Marian Mass every Saturday and, a little later, a daily office in honor of the Blessed Virgin. This Office of Mary became a supplement to the standard Divine Office and paralleled each of its eight "hours." It was prayed, privately or publicly, just before or after each current hour of the Office.

Like so many devotions that grew up in monasteries, the Marian Office soon spread, by way of imitation, to cathedral churches, parish churches, third orders, confraternities and sororities, and other forms of pious association.

In the beginning (ninth and tenth centuries), the daily Office of the Virgin was almost invariable. It had the same hymns, psalms, canticles, and prayers every day of the year, taken largely from the Common of Virgins, and its readings were usually cast in the form of prayers to the Virgin. In many monasteries and cathedrals where this devotion flourished—often in a special lady-chapel attached to the main church—the daily Office of Mary and her daily Mass persisted in this unvarying form century after century. This held true, for example, for the Marian Office that persisted among the Cistercians (Trappists), Dominicans, and Carmelites until the mid-twentieth century.

At Rome itself, however, and especially in the chapel of the papal household where the pope and his staff celebrated the daily office, the Marian Office took on a somewhat different character. There the lessons at Matins were always chosen from scripture and along with some appropriate antiphons and prayers gave a seasonal flavor at least to Advent and Christmas. At the prompting of St. Francis of Assisi (1180–1226), this Marian Office was adopted by the early Franciscans, and was carried far and wide throughout the Latin Church by these indefatigable preachers and teachers. They also suggested its use to the members of the Third Order of Penance and this popularized it among the laity to a considerable degree.

By the thirteenth century, the Office of Mary became the chief component of the Books of Hours that proved to be the historical origin of all the popular prayer books of the Latin Church. In Latin or the vernacular the Books of Hours appealed to the literate laity and were often beautifully bound and illustrated. Almost every North American museum holds one or more magnificently illuminated Book of Hours that is a testimonial to the devotion and artistic skills of our ancestors. The Cleveland Art Museum, for example, possesses a particularly fine example in the Book of Hours that once belonged to Queen Isabella the Catholic, the patroness of Christopher Columbus.

In the sixteenth century, the Roman form of the Office of Mary continued to appear in the reformed Breviary of 1568 although it was no longer obligatory for the clergy. From the sixteenth to the twentieth century, however, "The Little Office of the Blessed Virgin Mary," as it came to be called, became ever more popular in the many new religious orders devoted to the corporal and spiritual works of mercy and among the more devout laity.

The drawback of the Roman Little Office was that it remained almost completely invariable in its psalms, hymns, canticles, and lessons and only took on some seasonal flavor during the seasons of Advent and Christmas. With the success of the liturgical movements of the nineteenth and twentieth centuries, such a daily office proved less and less satisfying. It became clear that what was wanted was a Marian Office that was reasonably brief, easy to use, richer in traditional elements, and more closely aligned with the church's year.

In response to such desires, and after he defined the dogma of the Assumption of Mary in 1950, Pope Pius XII asked the Jesuit scripture scholar Augustine Bea—later a Roman cardinal and leading ecumenist at the Second Vatican Council—to increase the variable elements of the Marian Office. Its structure and length were to remain the same, but additional hymns, antiphons for the psalms and canticles, readings, and prayers would highlight the seasons of both Advent-Christmas and Lent-Easter.

This enlarged and improved office had only a brief history. Because of a variety of competing office books in the vernacular just before the Council and the appearance of the new Liturgy of the Hours in 1970, the Little Office of Mary just about disappeared in the maelstrom of counterproposals that ensued.

Structures of the Office

The Little Office proposed here is simple, brief, and invariable in *structure*. It has three times of prayer (hours) each day:

1. Morning Prayer (Lauds) to open and sanctify the day of work and prayer. It includes a hymn, one or more

psalms, a short reading, a canticle, and prayers of intercession.

2. Evening Prayer (Vespers) to close the work day and prepare for the night. It has the same elements as Morning Prayer and will be especially useful for families and communities at the end of the day.

3. An Hour of Readings modeled on the ancient Night Vigil and inspired by the improvements introduced by the Second Vatican Council: fewer psalms and a wider choice of readings. It will prove most useful for those with more time for daily prayer: the retired, older people, shut-ins, the bedridden, and insomniacs, and may be prayed at any hour of the day or night.

These hours are brief and simply structured. Morning and Evening Prayer will require only some fifteen minutes; even the Hour of Readings will take only around twenty minutes, depending on the time allowed for meditation on the readings. They are heavily seasonal in character, with the full flavor of the five liturgical seasons. And they are contained in one small, portable book.

Finally, this is a prayer book focused entirely on Jesus and Mary as they live through the mysteries of the incarnation, passion, death, and resurrection of Christ our Lord and their striking reflections in the dormition, assumption, and coronation of "the great Mother of God, Mary most holy."

Suggestions for Praying the Office

"Through Jesus let us continually offer a sacrifice of praise to God, that is, the fruit of lips that confess his name. Do not neglect to do good and to share what you have, for such sacrifices are pleasing to God" (Hebrews 13:15).

This prayer book is designed to be used by either one person praying alone or by groups of praying Christians. The following suggestions will help us do this effectively and in the spirit of the above quotation.

In solo recitation, a person should feel free to stand, sit, or kneel during an hour, but should make the sign of the cross where it is indicated (+) and bow during doxologies, that is, wherever the Blessed Trinity is honored by the "Glory to the Father" or by a doxology at the close of a hymn. The meditative pauses after the psalms, reading, and intercessory prayer are an essential part of the hour but may be lengthened at the devotion of the user.

In group prayer, the following suggestions are traditional and provide an easy, gentle, and unhurried way of praying:

1. Community prayer needs a *leader* of prayer and a *reader* for the lesson(s).

The group may divide into two sides ("choirs") for the praying of the hymns, canticles, and psalms; the first side says the first set of verses (stanza) and the second side responds with the second stanza. Or, more simply, the leader may be the first side and the whole group the second side.

Wherever the sign of the cross (+) appears in the text, all should sign themselves with the full sign of the cross. Whenever a doxology appears—whether the "Glory to the Father" at the end of a psalm or canticle or in the final stanza of a hymn—everyone should bow in honor of the Blessed Trinity, the end and aim of all our prayer.

A kiss of peace may be exchanged at the end of each hour, especially at Evening Prayer; it may take the form of an actual kiss, an embrace, or a handshake.

Posture: *Standing* is for the opening versicles and hymn and for the canticle after the reading. *Sitting* is appropriate for the psalm and the reading(s). *Kneeling* is the normal posture for the litanies of petition and for the blessing at the end of each hour.

2. All group prayer should begin with a few moments of silent, concentrated prayer to the God of all inspiration who makes our prayer possible and profitable. The Jesus Prayer is especially recommended for this purpose.

3. The designated leader of prayer—for example, the mother or father in family prayer—says the opening versicle and all make the response. The leader does the same with the versicle after the reading and initiates each Antiphon up to the asterisk. The whole group responds in unison with the second versicle and continues an Antiphon to the end. When an Antiphon is repeated after a psalm or canticle, everyone recites it in unison. The leader also says the psalm prayer, leads the litany and its concluding prayer, and asks the blessing at the end of each hour. The directions (rubrics) that appear in the season of Advent, pages 33-56, are indicators for the whole year.

4. Pauses for silent meditation after the psalm and the Reading, and for spontaneous prayer at the end of each litany are of the first importance for both personal and group prayer. It is the leader's role to bring such a pause to a suitable end. Too long a pause breaks the rhythm of group prayer; too short a pause is of little spiritual value. See St. Benedict's advice below.

5. Group prayer can be ruined by haste and by a lack of respect for the structure of hymns, psalms, and canticles. They are poems with a rhythm and balance of their own that demands attention and has to be learned by experience in using them. Rushing

through them unnerves any group of worshipers and destroys the atmosphere of devotion that is required for sound prayer. Much of the distaste for communal prayer surely stems from the haste that destroys recollection and devotion. A visit to a devout monastery or an experienced prayer group is the best way to appreciate how to pace group prayer. Chant discs will also help us in getting the flavor and style for praying the poetry of the office.

6. Finally, we must admit that even these brief "hours" will seem too long for some people, especially beginners. Quality, not quantity, is the name of the game. To select and pray any part of an hour with care is far more spiritually rewarding than hurrying through the whole thing. We would not want to hear the reproach: "These people draw near with their mouths and honor me with their lips, but their hearts are far from me" (Isaiah 29:13).

The spiritual advice of St. Benedict of Nursia (ca. 480–547) is helpful here:

Chapter 19: The Discipline of Psalmody

We believe that the divine presence is everywhere and *that in every place the eyes of the Lord are watching the good and the wicked* (Proverbs 15:3). But beyond the least doubt we should believe this to be especially true when we celebrate the divine office.

We must always remember, therefore, what the prophet says: *Serve the Lord with fear* (Psalm 2:11), and again, *Sing praise wisely* (Psalm 47:8); and, *In the presence of the angels I will sing to you* (Psalm 138:1). Let us consider, then, how we ought to behave in the presence of God and the angels, and let us stand to sing the psalms in such a way that our minds are in harmony with our voices.

Chapter 20: Reverence in Prayer

Whenever we want to ask some favor of a powerful person, we do it humbly and respectfully, for fear of presumption. How much more important, then, to lay our petitions before the Lord God of all things with the utmost humility and sincere devotion. We must know that God regards our purity of heart and tears of compunction, not our many words. Prayer should therefore be short and pure, unless perhaps it is prolonged under the inspiration of divine grace. In community, however, prayer should always be brief; and when the superior gives the signal, all should rise together.[4]

Psalms and Canticles in Christian Usage

Many people find the use of so many psalms and Old Testament canticles in a Christian prayer book to be a difficulty. They may know that the Book of Psalms was actually the hymn book of the Second Temple and was used in synagogue worship, and in the Jewish home, for example by Jesus, Mary, and Joseph. They may also know by reading the New Testament that the psalms are often quoted in it. They also play a large role in the celebration of the Eucharist and even more in the Liturgy of the Hours. Nevertheless, since they are all part of the old dispensation and do not seem to speak clearly of Jesus and Mary, how can we make a Christian use of the psalms?[5]

What we have to appreciate is that, from the very beginning, Jesus, the apostles, and the writers of the New Testament understood that the psalms and canticles spoke of Christ, the gospel, and the whole mission of the church. For them they spoke not so much of the past but of the present. In the events and personalities of our Jewish past we can discern with the eyes of faith their fuller meaning as it is revealed in Jesus. That means that the Old Testament is more than the history of our past; it prefigures, predicts, prophesies, and expresses Christ and the church.

Very early on the church not only continued to use the psalms in its worship but did so in a specifically

Christian way. It dropped the old Hebrew titles for the psalms and substituted new interpretive ones that brought them into the Christian present. For example, with a new title, an accompanying antiphon, and a psalm prayer, Psalm 2 can be appropriated in a fully Christian sense. See pages 61-62 of Morning Prayer for Christmas. What was once—literally and historically—a royal poem that spoke of the choice and coronation of a king of Israel and of his victorious reign, now becomes a description of God's chosen Son, our messianic King and Prince of Peace. Psalm 2 had already been appropriated in the New Testament in that way and therefore set a precedent for its use in the liturgy and in private prayer.

Not only could many psalms be adapted in that way, St. Augustine of Hippo (354–430), the greatest Latin exegete of the Bible, thought that *every* psalm spoke of Christ in some way and that the psalter was the Christian hymn book *par excellence.* Perhaps that is why other forms of hymnody were rather slow to come to birth in the nascent church. It already had one hundred and fifty psalms and numerous Old Testament canticles to use in its worship.

If we want to enjoy the use of the psalms in our prayer, we have to both respect their literal/historical meanings and also learn how to use them precisely as Christians. This Office of Mary builds on that tradition and employs the kind of titles, antiphons, and psalm prayers that facilitate their accommodation to Marian prayer. It even suggests a further step that may disconcert some. Some early Christians inserted new words into a psalm in order to bring out its fuller meaning. An example: Psalm 96:10 has in Hebrew: "Say among the nations, 'The Lord reigns.'" But in the early Latin psalters the same line reads: "Dicite in gentibus quia Dominus regnavit *a ligno*"; "Say among the nations, The Lord reigns *from the tree.*" The medieval and Tridentine Latin liturgy used this line all through the Season of Easter to emphasize the role of the victorious cross of Christ.

Many of the psalms and canticles in this book can be accommodated in a Marian sense. See Psalm 67, line 1 in Advent, pages 38-39. The mental addition of the one word "Jesus" in the first line would bring out a fresh sense of the importance of this text in an Advent liturgy. See the Canticle of Zephaniah, line 2, page 40, where a substitution like "O Mary of Nazareth" for "O Israel" would specify the sense and use of this text. See Psalm 147b, line 2, page 41, where "O Mary!" may replace "O Zion!" These accommodations are examples of how it might become easier for many people to catch the fuller meaning of these venerable texts in a Marian context. In this way we can accomplish with the Psalter what Jesus affirmed so emphatically about the Old Testament in general: "Do not think that I have come to abolish the law or the prophets; I have come not to abolish but to fulfill.

For truly I tell you, until heaven and earth pass away, not one letter, not one stroke of a letter, will pass from the law until all is accomplished" (Matthew 5:17-18).

Those who pray the psalms and canticles within such a Catholic tradition will learn how to accommodate more and more of them in this way without difficulty. It is all a matter of "seeing Christ" in the psalms. To cite an old maxim: "What lies hidden in the Old Testament shines forth in the New."

Notes

1. *Homilies in Praise of the Blessed Virgin Mary.* Homily 4.1. Trans Marie Bernard Said, Cistercian Fathers Series, 18A (Kalamazoo, MI: Cistercian Pub., 1993), p. 45.

2. The Latin text of this hymn is as follows:

    > Sub tuum praesidium confugimus,
    > sancta Dei Genetrix.
    > Nostras deprecationes ne despicias in
    > necessitatibus,
    > sed a periculis cunctis libera nos semper,
    > Virgo gloriosa et benedicta.

    A Book of Prayers (Washington, DC: International Commission on English in the Liturgy, 1982).

3. G. G. Meersseman, O.P., ed. and trans., *The Akathistos Hymn* (Fribourg, Switz.: The University Press, 1958); another very poetic translation was made by Vincent McNabb, O.P., *Ode in Honor of the Holy Immaculate Most Blessed and Glorious Lady Mother of God and Ever Virgin Mary* (Oxford: Blackfriars, 1947). McNabb thought it was composed by Romanus the Singer (ca. 490-ca. 560) but it is considerably older than that. A translation of the *Akathist* by Lazarus Moore appears in St. John Maximovitch, *The Orthodox Veneration of Mary, the Birthgiver of God* (Platina, CA: St. Herman of Alaska Brotherhood, 1996, 5th ed.). A Greek text

with an English translation by N. Michael Vaporis is available from Themely Publications, 25 Hewitt Circle, Needhan, MS 02194.

4. *The Rule of St. Benedict in English*, trans. Timothy Fry, O.S.B. (Collegeville, MN: The Liturgical Press, 1982). Commentators on the *Holy Rule* agree that the "prayer" in question here refers to the pauses for silent prayer after the psalms. This advice on brevity is equally applicable to the pause after the Readings and for the pause for spontaneous prayer at the end of the litany.

5. Thomas Merton's *Bread in the Wilderness* (New Directions, 1953) gives a fine explanation of the psalms in Christian use. It has been reprinted by The Liturgical Press, Collegeville, MN.

$\mathcal{T}$ABLE OF

MOVABLE

FEASTS

$\mathcal{T}$he first Sunday in Advent is the beginning of the church's year of grace. It falls some four weeks before Christmas day. Christmas is, of course, a fixed feast (December 25), but Ash Wednesday and Pentecost are movable feasts and depend entirely on the variable date of Easter. A table of such days is needed to locate the beginning of Advent, Lent, Easter, and Assumptiontide.

YEAR	Ash Wed.	Easter	Pentecost	Advent
2002	13 February	31 March	19 May	1 December
2003	5 March	20 April	8 June	30 November
2004	25 February	11 April	30 May	28 November
2005	9 February	27 March	15 May	27 November
2006	1 March	16 April	4 June	3 December
2007	21 February	8 April	27 May	2 December
2008	6 February	23 March	11 May	30 November
2009	25 February	12 April	31 May	29 November
2010	17 February	4 April	23 May	28 November
2011	9 March	24 April	12 June	27 November
2012	22 February	8 April	27 May	2 December
2013	13 February	31 March	19 May	1 December
2014	5 March	20 April	8 June	30 November
2015	18 February	5 April	24 May	29 November
2016	10 February	27 March	15 May	27 November
2017	1 March	16 April	4 June	3 December
2018	14 February	1 April	20 May	2 December
2019	6 March	21 April	9 June	1 December
2020	26 February	12 April	31 May	30 November

(Information courtesy of the Rev. Peter D. Rocca, C.S.C., Rector of Sacred Heart Basilica, the University of Notre Dame.)

The Marian

Liturgical

Year

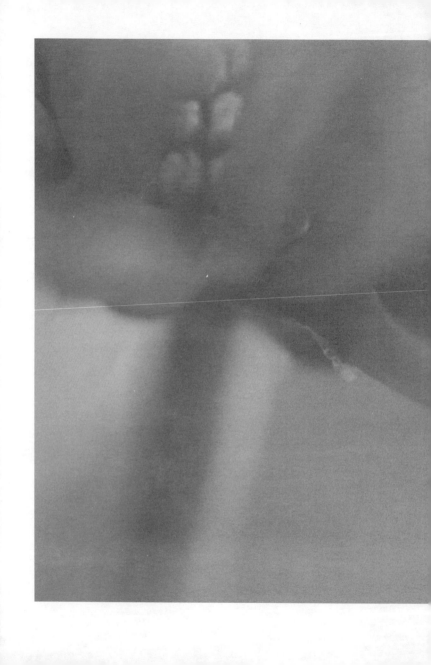

ℐHE SEASON OF ADVENT

Advent is a season for celebrating the first and second comings of our Lord and our Lady's role in them both. Jesus came at first in humility and he will come again in glory at the end of time.

He came the first time as the Son of the eternal Father in our flesh and blood through the free consent of a human Mother; he came as God among us, Emmanuel, God-with-us. But his greatest promise is that he will come again in glory—in his transfigured humanity—to judge the living and the dead.

Jesus is, of course, the very center of the whole gospel story. But Mary is the first member of the great supporting cast of these world-shaking events. She is the indispensable Mother of the new Adam and of the new order which his incarnation inaugurates. To understand her magnificent role, we have only to glance at her as she appears over and over again in Christian art down through the ages: the images of the Roman catacombs; the magnificent mosaics of the great fifth-century church— St. Mary Major—in downtown Rome; the mosaics of Hagia Sophia (Holy Wisdom), the cathedral church of Constantinople; the icons of the Christian East, the frescoes and mosaics of medieval churches, even the cribs and cards of a modern Christmas. Who is central in each picture? Mary as the Seat of Wisdom, Mary as the Mother of the God-Man, presenting him to believers and to all the world for its adoration and obedience.

Mary is the Lady of the First Coming, of the Incarnation, of the Church. In a special way Mary is our Lady of the Blessed Sacrament since she supplied the very body and blood that we feed upon and adore in the eucharist. Her shrines throughout the world—Lourdes, Fatima, Guadalupe, and so many others—are the perpetual goal of numberless pilgrimages. In the church Mary's influence is all-pervading: theology, prayer, feasts, devotions, piety, local and international shrines.

She is the great attendant of our Savior in all his activity on our behalf and truly our *Alma mater*: the affectionate and loving Mother of all who believe in Jesus. In a very special way she is the mother of the poor, the downtrodden, and the persecuted. As set out in her *Magnificat* (Luke 1:46-55), her mission is to assist in the overthrow of all worldly values, to upset all merely secular points of view and, above all, to "scatter the proud in their conceit, cast down the mighty from their thrones, lift up the lowly, fill the hungry with good things and send the rich away empty."

Mary is also our Lady of the Second Coming. Her single purpose, in the eternity she shares body and soul with Christ her Son, is preparing the whole church and each individual Christian for the *parousia* (the Second Coming). When Christ comes again in glory on the clouds of heaven, she will accompany him as Queen. Not without reason do we pray continuously: "Holy Mary, Mother of God, pray for us sinners, now and at the hour of our death"—and at the Last Judgment.

Besides Mary, other significant figures people the Advent scene. First there is the Archangel Gabriel who comes as the messenger of the Most High to Mary of Nazareth; he asks her to accept in faith the mission and destiny of being the mother of the Messiah. Then there is Mary's cousin Elizabeth who "exclaims with a loud cry: 'Blessed are you among women, and blessed is the fruit of your womb'" (Luke 1:42). Elizabeth is the mother of John the Baptist who leaps with joy in her womb when Mary greets her. John the Baptist is the herald of the Messiah and of God's reign as he baptized Jesus in the River Jordan. Another personage is St. Joseph, the husband of Mary. An angel appears to him too and tells him not to be afraid to take an already pregnant Mary to be his bride. All these figures prepare us for the mystery of Christmas and the further unfolding of who Jesus is and what the kingdom of God will be like.

It is important to remind ourselves that the liturgy of Advent—and of all the seasons—is not just a commemoration of past events. Rather, these wonderful happenings recorded in the Bible are present, saving events in the sacraments of the church and a real anticipation of all God's promises and their fulfillment at the end of time.

The season of Advent is roughly four weeks long; it begins the Sunday on or nearest the feast of St. Andrew the Apostle (November 30) and lasts until Christmas Eve (December 24); see the Table of Movable Feasts, page 30.

Advent Morning Prayer

Leader:	O God, + come to my assistance.
All:	—O Lord, make haste to help me.
Leader:	Hail, Mary, full of grace,
All:	—The Lord is with you.
Leader:	Blessed are you among women,
All:	—And blessed is the fruit of your womb, Jesus.
Leader:	Holy Mary, Mother of God, pray for us sinners,
All:	—Now and at the hour of our death. Amen.

Hymn

1. God the Father sends his angel
   from his throne in heaven above;
   when the angel speaks to Mary,
   Mary's heart is full of love.

2. Gabriel says: "Rejoice, O Mary,
   full of grace: the Lord is near.
   You will bear God's Son, O Maiden:
   God has promised, have no fear."

3. Mary says: "I am God's servant;
   I will keep his holy word;

I will gladly be the Mother
of my Savior and my Lord."

4. Now the Spirit overshadows
   God the Father's chosen one:
   She becomes the Maiden-Mother
   of the Father's only Son.

5. God the Word, the Father's Wisdom,
   comes on earth as Mary's child:
   God, our glory, shines among us;
   God with us is reconciled.

6. Praise the Father, fount of blessing;
   praise his Son, whom Mary bore;
   praise the Lord of life, the Spirit;
   praise one God for evermore. Amen.

Text: James Quinn, S.J.

Pray one or more of the following three psalms.

Psalm 67
Praise the Messiah, Mary's Son

Antiphon   Let the peoples praise you, O God; *
                 let all the peoples praise you.

1. O God be gracious and bless us
   and let your face shed its light upon us.
   So will your ways be known upon earth
   and all nations learn your saving help.

2. Let the peoples praise you, O God;
   let all the peoples praise you.

3. Let the nations be glad and exult
   for you rule the world with justice.
   With fairness you rule the peoples,
   you guide the nations on earth.

4. Let the peoples praise you, O God;
   let all the peoples praise you.

5. The earth has yielded its fruit
   for God, our God, has blessed us.
   May God still give us blessing
   till the ends of the earth stand in awe.

Antiphon   Let the peoples praise you, O God;
               let all the peoples praise you.

Psalm Prayer

Leader: Let us pray *(pause for silent prayer)*.
Blessed Mother of our Savior,
open the gates of revelation
to every nation on earth
that the world may shout for joy
and praise the name of Jesus,
now and always and for ever and ever.
All: —Amen.

Canticle of Zephaniah 3:14-18

Antiphon   You are the bright * and the morning star,
            O Christ our Lord.

1. Sing aloud, O daughter of Zion;
    shout, O Israel!
    Rejoice and exult with all your heart,
    O daughter of Jerusalem!
    The LORD has taken away the judgments against you,
    he has turned away your enemies.

2. The king of Israel, the LORD, is in your midst;
    you shall fear disaster no more.
    On that day it shall be said to Jerusalem:
    Do not fear, O Zion;
    do not let your hands grow weak.
    The LORD, your God, is in your midst,
    a warrior who gives victory.

Antiphon   You are the bright and the morning star,
            O Christ our Lord.

Prayer

Leader: Let us pray *(pause for silent prayer)*.
To enlighten the world, O God,
you sent us your Word
as the sun of truth and justice.
Illumine our minds,

renew us in your love
and make us shout for joy;
through Christ Jesus our Savior.
All:　　　—Amen.

Psalm 147b Jerusalem the Golden

Antiphon　Great city of God, * Mary most holy!

1. O praise the Lord, Jerusalem!
   Zion, praise your God!

2. For God has strengthened the bars of your gates,
   and has blessed the children within you;
   has established peace on your borders,
   and feeds you with the finest wheat.

3. God sends out word to the earth
   and swiftly runs the command.
   God showers down snow white as wool,
   and scatters hoarfrost like ashes.

4. God hurls down hailstones like crumbs,
   and causes the waters to freeze.
   God sends forth a word and it melts them:
   at the breath of God's mouth the waters flow.

5. God makes his word known to Jacob,
   to Israel his laws and decrees.
   God has not dealt thus with other nations;
   has not taught them divine decrees.

6. Glory to the Father, and to the Son,
   and to the Holy Spirit:

7. as it was in the beginning, is now,
   and will be for ever. Amen.

Antiphon   Great city of God, Mary most holy!

Reading: God the Restorer
Romans 1:1-4

Paul, a servant of Jesus Christ, called to be an apostle, set apart for the gospel of God, which he promised beforehand through his prophets in the holy scriptures, the gospel concerning his Son, who was descended from David according to the flesh and was declared to be Son of God with power according to the spirit of holiness by resurrection from the dead, Jesus Christ our Lord.

Pause for meditation.

Response

Leader: A Virgin shall conceive and bear a Son,
          alleluia!

All: —And she shall call his name Emmanuel,
          alleluia!

Canticle of Zachary
Luke 1:68-79

Antiphon   Drop down dew, heavens from above; *
                let the earth bud forth a Savior.

1. Now + bless the God of Israel,
   Who comes in love and power,
   Who raises from the royal house
   Deliverance in this hour.

2. Through holy prophets God has sworn
   To free us from alarm,
   To save us from the heavy hand
   Of all who wish us harm.

3. Remembering the covenant,
   God rescues us from fear,
   That we might serve in holiness
   And peace from year to year.

4. And you, my child, shall go before
   To preach, to prophesy,
   That all may know the tender love,
   The grace of God most high.

5. In tender mercy, God will send
   The dayspring from on high,
   Our rising sun, the light of life
   For those who sit and sigh.

6. God comes to guide our way to peace,
   That death shall reign no more.
   Sing praises to the Holy One!
   O worship and adore!

Text: *Benedictus,* trans. Ruth Duck

Antiphon   Drop down dew, heavens from above;
            let the earth bud forth a Savior.

Litany

Leader: Let us pray to the Lord who is coming to
            save us:

All: —Come and save us.
            Lord Jesus, Anointed One of God,
            —Come and save us.
            You came forth from the Father into our
            world,
            —Come and save us.
            You were conceived by the overshadowing
            Spirit,
            —Come and save us.
            You took flesh in the womb of the Virgin
            Mary,
            —Come and save us.
            Lord and Savior of the living and the dead,
            —Come and save us.

Spontaneous prayers of intercession

Closing Prayer

Leader: God of love and mercy,
help us to follow the example of Mary,
always ready to do your will.
At the message of an angel
she welcomed your eternal Son
and, filled with the light of your Spirit,
she became the temple of your Word,
who lives and reigns with you and the Holy Spirit,
one God, for ever and ever.
All: —Amen.

Opening Prayer for December 20, *The Roman Missal.*

Blessing

Leader: May Christ, Son of God and Son of Mary
+ bless us and keep us.
All: —Amen.

A Marian Poem

I sing of a Maiden
of matchless perfection:
King of all kings
for her Son she chose.

He came all so still
where his Mother was,
as fine dew in April
that falls on the grass.

He came all so still
to his Mother's bower,
as soft dew in April
that falls on the flower.

He came all so still
where his Mother lay,
as sweet dew in April
that falls on the spray.

Mother and Maiden
was never none but she;
Well may such a Lady
God's own Mother be!

Anon., 15th century, alt.

Advent Evening Prayer

Leader:	O God, + come to my assistance.
All:	—O Lord, make haste to help me.
Leader:	Hail, Mary, full of grace,
All:	—The Lord is with you.
Leader:	Blessed are you among women,
All:	—And blessed is the fruit of your womb, Jesus.
Leader:	Holy Mary, Mother of God, pray for us sinners,
All:	—Now and at the hour of our death. Amen.

Hymn

1. Mother of Christ, our hope, our patroness,
   Star of the sea, our beacon in distress,
   Guide to the shores of everlasting day
   God's holy people on their pilgrim way.

2. Virgin, in you God made his dwelling place;
   Mother of all the living, full of grace,
   Blessed are you: God's word you did believe;
   "Yes" on your lips undid the "No" of Eve.

3. Daughter of God, who bore his holy One,
   Dearest of all to Christ, your loving Son,

Show us his face, O Mother, as on earth,
Loving us all, you gave our Savior birth.

Text: Alma Redemptoris Mater, trans. James Quinn, S.J.

Pray one or more of the following three psalms.

Psalm 110   The Messiah Priest-King

Antiphon   The angel Gabriel * brought the message to
Mary and she conceived by the Holy Spirit.

1. The LORD's revelation to my Master:
    "Sit on my right;
    your foes I will put beneath your feet."

2. The LORD will wield from Zion
    your scepter of power;
    rule in the midst of all your foes.

3. A prince from the day of your birth
    on the holy mountains;
    from the womb before the dawn I begot you.

4. The LORD has sworn an oath and will not change.
    "You are a priest for ever,
    a priest like Melchizedek of old."

5. The Master standing at your right hand
    will shatter rulers in the day of wrath,

6. Will judge all the nations,
    will heap high the bodies;
    heads shall be scattered far and wide.

7. He shall drink from the stream by the wayside,
    will stand with head held high.

Antiphon   The Angel Gabriel brought the message to
             Mary and she conceived by the Holy Spirit.

Psalm Prayer

Leader: Let us pray *(pause for silent prayer)*.
Loving Father,
you show the world the splendor of your glory
in the coming of Christ, born of the Virgin.
By her merits and prayers make us worthy
to celebrate the mystery of the Incarnation;
through the same Christ our Lord.
All: —Amen.

Psalm 112 Happy Is Mary

Antiphon   I am the Lord's servant; *
             let it happen as God wills.

1. Happy are those who fear the LORD,
    who take delight in all God's commands.
    Their descendants shall be powerful on earth;
    the children of the upright are blessed.

2. Wealth and riches are in their homes;
    their justice stands firm for ever.
    They are lights in the darkness for the upright;
    they are generous, merciful and just.

3. Good people take pity and lend,
    they conduct their affairs with honor.
    The just will never waver,
    they will be remembered for ever.

4. They have no fear of evil news;
    with firm hearts they trust in the LORD.
    With steadfast hearts they will not fear;
    they will see the downfall of their foes.

5. Openhanded, they give to the poor;
    their justice stands firm for ever.
    Their heads will be raised in glory.

6. The wicked shall see this and be angry,
    shall grind their teeth and pine away;
    the desires of the wicked lead to doom.

Antiphon   I am the Lord's servant; let it happen as
            God wills.

Psalm Prayer

Leader: Let us pray *(pause for silent prayer)*.
God of mercy and justice,
you shone on the darkness of our world
by choosing Mary of Nazareth
to be the mother of your Son.
Make us steady and fearless in his service

with steadfast hearts that love God,
now and for ever.

All: —Amen.

Canticle of Simeon
Luke 2:29-32

Antiphon   The Child to be born * will be called the
            Son of God.

1. Now, Lord, you let your servant go in peace,
    your word has been fulfilled:

2. My own eyes have seen the salvation
    which you have prepared in the sight of every
        people:

3. a light to reveal you to the nations
    and the glory of your people Israel.

4. Glory to the Father, and to the Son,
    and to the Holy Spirit:

5. as it was in the beginning, is now,
    and will be for ever. Amen.

Text: *English Language Liturgical Consultation*

Antiphon   The Child to be born will be called the Son
            of God.

Reading: The Time of the Messiah
Isaiah 35:1-2

The wilderness and the dry land shall be glad,
the desert shall rejoice and blossom;
like the crocus it shall blossom abundantly,
and rejoice with joy and singing.

The glory of Lebanon shall be given to it,
and the majesty of Carmel and Sharon.
They shall see the glory of the LORD,
the majesty of our God.

Pause for meditation.

Response

Leader:	Blessed are you among women, O Mary,
All:	—And blessed is the fruit of your womb, Jesus.

Canticle of the Blessed Virgin Mary
Luke 1:46-55

Antiphon   What the virgin Eve * bound fast through unbelief, the Virgin Mary set free through faith.

1. My soul + proclaims the greatness of the Lord.
    My spirit sings to God, my saving God,

Who on this day above all others favored me
And raised me up, a light for all to see.

2. Through me great deeds will God make manifest,
   And all the earth will come to call me blest.
   Unbounded love and mercy sure will I proclaim
   For all who know and praise God's holy name.

3. God's mighty arm, protector of the just,
   Will guard the weak and raise them from the dust.
   But mighty kings will swiftly fall from thrones
       corrupt,
   The strong brought low, the lowly lifted up.

4. Soon will the poor and hungry of the earth
   Be richly blest, be given greater worth.
   And Israel, as once foretold to Abraham,
   Will live in peace throughout the promised land.

5. All glory be to God, Creator blest,
   To Jesus Christ, God's love made manifest,
   And to the Holy Spirit, gentle Comforter,
   All glory be, both now and evermore. Amen.

Text: *Magnificat*, trans. Owen Alstott.

Antiphon   What the virgin Eve bound fast through
           unbelief, the Virgin Mary set free through
           faith.

A Litany of the Blessed Virgin Mary

(see pages 299-308)

Spontaneous prayers of intercession

Closing Prayer

Leader: Father, all-powerful God,
your eternal Word took flesh on our earth
when the Virgin Mary placed her life
at the service of your plan.
Lift our minds in watchful hope
to hear the voice which announces his glory
and open our minds to receive the Spirit
who prepares us for his coming.
We ask this through Christ our Lord.
All: —Amen.

Alternate Opening Prayer for the Fourth Sunday of Advent *The Roman Missal.*

Blessing

Leader: May the Virgin Mary mild
                 + bless us with her holy Child.
All: —Amen.

A sign of peace may be exchanged.

The Proclamation of the Nativity

Many ages after the creation of the world,
when in the beginning God made the heavens and the
    earth,
long after the flood and the primeval covenant made
    with Noah,
more than two thousand years after the promises
made to our father Abraham and our mother Sarah,
fifteen centuries after Moses and Miriam and the
    Exodus from Egypt,
one thousand years after David was anointed king of
    Israel,
in the sixty-fifth week according to the prophecy of
    Daniel,
in the one hundred and ninety-fourth Olympiad,
in the year seven-hundred and fifty-two from the
    founding of Rome,
in the forty-second year of the emperor Octavian
    Augustus Caesar,
and in the sixth age of the world,
while the whole earth lay in peace,
in order to consecrate the world by his gracious coming,

JESUS THE CHRIST,

eternal God and Son of the everlasting Father,
conceived in time by the overshadowing
of the Holy Spirit,
nine months having elapsed since his conception,

was born of the Virgin Mary in Bethlehem of Judea,

GOD MADE MAN.

This is the birthday according to the flesh of
our Lord Jesus Christ.

The Roman Martyrology, alt.

THE SEASON OF CHRISTMAS

Christmas is the extension and the fulfillment of Advent. More figures surround and magnify the incarnate Son of God: the angels of the Bethlehem skies singing "Glory to God in the highest" and the lowly shepherds at the crib; later the mysterious Magi from the East with their precious and prophetic gifts; King Herod and the innocent babes of Bethlehem. Finally, there are the holy pair of ancient ascetics, Simeon and Anna, in the Temple when Jesus, Mary, and Joseph appear to fulfill the law of Moses. Last of all, there is John the Baptist, the ultimate Old Testament prophet and forerunner of the Messiah whom he baptized in the Jordan. With John, the Messianic era really comes into being and readies us for the life, death, and resurrection of the Lord Jesus and the fullness of the kingdom of God.

Before Christ, December 25 was the winter solstice of the Julian calendar. It was also the feast of "the Sun God that never dies" (*sol invictus*) because it was reborn each year at the winter solstice. This cult had spread far and wide since the late third century and had been adopted in a special way by the dynasty of the Emperor Constantine (306–337). The Christian feast of Christ's birth was first celebrated at Rome some time before 336 AD, when it is first mentioned in a Roman calendar. The Church of Rome probably chose to celebrate the nativity on the winter solstice for several reasons: to tie it into the turning of the seasons and the coming of new light; out of deference to the Emperor Constantine who was favoring and fostering Christianity rather than persecuting it; as a liturgical memorial to the Council of Nicaea (325) which had proclaimed the full divinity of Christ; and, then, for a more ancient and profound reason. Very early on and long before the creation of Christmas or Good Friday, March 25 had been considered as both the annual commemoration of Mary's conception of Jesus and of his death on the cross. December 25, coming nine months after his conception, would be the exact counterpart of March 25.

It was not long before Roman Christmas drew into its orbit the beautiful eastern feasts celebrating the manifestation of the Lord: Epiphany (January 6), the Baptism of Jesus, the wedding feast of Cana, and, finally, the Presentation of Jesus in the Temple, forty days after his birth (February 2).

After the Ecumenical Council of Ephesus (431) defended the unity of the person of the God-Man by proclaiming Mary as *Theotokos* (Mother of God), Pope Sixtus III erected the magnificent basilica of St. Mary Major in her honor and adorned it with splendid mosaics depicting her role in salvation history. Soon after the Pope began celebrating the main masses of Christmas in that central church. Later it was called St. Mary-at-the-Crib when relics of the crib of Bethlehem were brought to Rome and deposited in a kind of cave-shrine beneath the high altar.

The season of Christmas has traditionally extended for forty days: from December 25 through February 2, the feast of the Presentation of the Lord in the Temple.

Christmas Morning Prayer

O God, + come to my assistance.
—O Lord, make haste to help me.
Hail, Mary, full of grace,
—The Lord is with you.
Blessed are you among women,
—And blessed is the fruit of your womb, Jesus.
Holy Mary, Mother of God, pray for us sinners,
—Now and at the hour of our death. Amen.

Hymn

1. Town of David, King and Shepherd,
    Now has come your promised hour,
    When the lowly branch of Jesse
    Blossoms into glorious flower.

2. Full of joy, the Virgin-Mother
    Now will bring her Lord to birth,
    Son of God and Son of Mary,
    God with us, a Child on earth.

3. After sin's long night of triumph
    Christ will dawn as endless day:
    Light of light, to heaven's glory
    He will guide our pilgrim way.

4. Sinless, he will die for sinners;
    wounded, he will be our peace;

poor, he will reward with riches;
captive, he will bring release.

5. Glory be to God the Father,
    Glory be to Mary's Child,
    Glory be to God the Spirit:
    God with us is reconciled. Amen.

Text: James Quinn, S.J.

Pray one or more of the following three psalms.

Psalm 2 God's Chosen Son

Antiphon   The Prince of Peace is exalted *
                 above all earth's rulers.

1. Why this tumult among nations,
    among peoples this useless murmuring?
    They arise, the kings of the earth,
    princes plot against the LORD and his Anointed.
    "Come, let break their fetters,
    come, let us cast off their yoke."

2. God who sits in the heavens laughs,
    the Lord is laughing them to scorn.
    Then God will speak in anger,
    and in rage will strike them with terror.
    "It is I who have set up my king
    on Zion my holy mountain."

3. I will announce the decree of the LORD.
   The Lord said to me: "You are my Son.
   It is I who have begotten you this day.
   Ask and I shall bequeath you the nations,
   put the ends of the earth in your possession.
   With a rod of iron you will break them,
   shatter them like a potter's jar."

4. Now, O kings, understand,
   take warning, rulers of the earth;
   serve the Lord with awe
   and trembling, pay your homage
   lest God be angry and you perish;
   for suddenly God's anger will blaze.

5. Blessed are they who put their trust in God.

Antiphon   The Prince of Peace is exalted
            above all earth's rulers.

Psalm Prayer

Let us pray *(pause for silent prayer)*.
God of power and life,
glory of all who believe in you,
fill the world with the splendor of Jesus,
the Prince of Peace,
and show the nations the light of truth.
We ask this through Christ our Lord.
—Amen.

Canticle of Micah 5:2-5
The Good Shepherd

Antiphon   He shall be called Emmanuel: *
               God-with-us.

1. You, O Bethlehem of Judea,
   who are one of the little clans of Judah,
   from you shall come forth for me
   one who is to rule in Israel,
   whose origin is from of old,
   from ancient days.

2. Therefore he shall give them up until the time
   when she who is in labor has brought forth;
   then the rest of his kindred shall return
   to the people of Israel.

3. And he shall stand and feed his flock
   in the strength of the Lord
   in the majesty of the name
   of the Lord his God.

4. And they shall live secure,
   for now he shall be great
   to the ends of the earth;
   and he shall be the one of peace.

Antiphon   He shall be called Emmanuel:
               God-with-us.

Prayer

Let us pray *(pause for silent prayer).*
Abba, our dear Father,
by the fruitful virginity of Blessed Mary
you conferred the benefits of everlasting salvation
upon the whole human race;
may we feel the power of her intercession
through whom we received the Author of life,
Jesus Christ our Lord.
—Amen.

Psalm 146 Our Faithful God

Antiphon   The time came for Mary *
            to deliver her Child, alleluia!

1. My soul gives praise to the LORD;
    I will praise the LORD all my days,
    make music to my God while I live.

2. Put no trust in the powerful,
    mere mortals, in whom there is no help.
    Take their breath, they return to clay
    and their plans that day come to nothing.

3. They are happy who are helped by Jacob's God,
    whose hope is in the LORD their God,
    who alone made heaven and earth,
    the seas and all they contain.

4. It is the Lord who keeps faith for ever,
    who is just to those who are oppressed.
    It is God who gives bread to the hungry,
    the LORD, who sets prisoners free,

5. the LORD who gives sight to the blind,
    who raises up those who are bowed down,
    the LORD, who protects the stranger
    and upholds the widow and orphan.

6. It is the LORD who loves the just
    but thwarts the path of the wicked.
    The LORD will reign for ever,
    Zion's God, from age to age.

7. Glory to the Father, and to the Son,
    and to the Holy Spirit:

8. as it was in the beginning, is now,
    and will be for ever. Amen.

Antiphon   The time came for Mary
            to deliver her Child, alleluia!

Reading: The Prince of Peace
Isaiah 9:6-7

A child has been born for us, a son given to us; authority rests upon his shoulders; and he is named Wonderful Counselor, Mighty God, Everlasting Father, Prince of Peace. His authority shall grow continually, and there shall be endless peace. . . . The zeal of the LORD of hosts will do this.

Pause for meditation.

Response

Here is a mystery beyond all telling, alleluia!
—The womb of the Virgin becomes the temple of God, alleluia!

The Canticle of the Angels
(*Gloria in excelsis Deo*)

Antiphon   The Word was made flesh, alleluia! *
             and dwelt among us, alleluia!

Or this Antiphon
             The Magi adored Christ *
             nursing at his Mother's breast, alleluia!
             The nations adore him,
             sitting at the right hand of the Father, alleluia!

1.   Glory to God in the highest,
    and peace to God's people on earth.

2.   Lord God, heavenly King,
    almighty God and Father,
    we worship you, we give you thanks,
    we praise you for your glory.

3. Lord Jesus Christ, only Son of the Father,
    Lord God, Lamb of God,
    you take away the sin of the world:
    have mercy on us;
    you are seated at the right hand of the Father:
    receive our prayer.

4. For you alone are the Holy One,
    you alone are the Lord,
    you alone are the Most High,
    Jesus Christ,
    with the Holy Spirit,
    in the glory of God the Father. Amen.

Text: *English Language Liturgical Consultation.*

One of the above antiphons is repeated.

Litany (Te Deum, part B)

You, Christ, are the king of glory,
—The eternal Son of the Father.
When you took our flesh to set us free
—You humbly chose the Virgin's womb.
You overcame the sting of death,
—And opened the kingdom of heaven to all believers.
You are seated at God's right hand in glory.
—We believe that you will come to be our judge.
Come, then, Lord, and help your people,

—Bought with the price of your own blood.
And bring us with your saints
—To glory everlasting.

Text: *English Language Liturgical Consultation.*

Spontaneous prayer

Closing Prayer

God our Father,
may we always profit by the prayers
of the Virgin Mother Mary,
for you bring us life and salvation
through Jesus Christ her Son,
who lives and reigns with you and the Holy Spirit,
one God, for ever and ever.
—Amen.

Opening Prayer for January 1, *The Roman Missal.*

Blessing

May the Word made flesh, the Son of Mary,
+ bless us and keep us.
—Amen.

The Shepherd Speaks

Out of the midnight sky a great dawn broke,
And a voice singing flooded us with song.
In David's city was He born, it sang,
A Savior, Christ the Lord. Then while I sat
Shivering with the thrill of that great cry,
A mighty choir a thousandfold more sweet
Suddenly sang, Glory to God and Peace—
Peace on the earth; my heart, almost unnerved
By that swift loveliness, would hardly beat.
Speechless we waited till the accustomed night
Gave us no promise more of sweet surprise;
Then scrambling to our feet, without a word
We started through the fields to find the Child.

John Erskine

Christmas Evening Prayer

O God, + come to my assistance.

—O Lord, make haste to help me.

Hail, Mary, full of grace,

—The Lord is with you.

Blessed are you among women,

—And blessed is the fruit of your womb, Jesus.

Holy Mary, Mother of God, pray for us sinners,

—Now and at the hour of our death. Amen.

Hymn

1. O Queen of heaven, to you the angels sing,
   The Maiden-Mother of their Lord and King;
   O Woman raised above the stars, receive
   The homage of your children, sinless Eve.

2. O full of grace, in grace your womb did bear
   Emmanuel, King David's promised heir;
   O Eastern Gate, whom God had made his own,
   By you God's glory came to Zion's throne.

3. O Burning Bush, you gave the world its light
   When Christ your Son was born on Christmas night;
   O Mary Queen, who bore God's holy One,
   For us, your children, pray to God your Son. Amen.

Text: *Ave, Regina caelorum*, trans. James Quinn, S.J.

Pray one or more of the following three psalms.

Psalm 46 God Is Always Near in Christ

Antiphon   Mary is the holy place *
                 where the Most High dwells, alleluia!

1.   God is for us a refuge and strength,
a helper close at hand, in time of distress,
so we shall not fear though the earth should rock,
though the mountains fall into the depths of the sea;
even though its waters rage and foam,
even though the mountains be shaken by its waves.

2.   The LORD of hosts is with us;
the God of Jacob is our refuge.

3.   The waters of a river give joy to God's city,
the holy place where the Most High dwells.
God is within, it cannot be shaken;
God will help it at the dawning of the day.
Nations are in tumult, kingdoms are shaken;
God's voice roars forth, the earth shrinks away.

4.   The LORD of hosts is with us;
the God of Jacob is our refuge.

5.   Come, consider the works of the LORD,
the redoubtable deeds God has done on earth:
putting an end to wars across the earth;
breaking the bow, snapping the spear;
burning the shields with fire.

"Be still and know that I am God,
supreme among the nations, supreme on the earth!"

6. The LORD of hosts is with us;
    the God of Jacob is our refuge.

Antiphon   Mary is the holy place
             where the Most High dwells, alleluia!

Psalm Prayer

Let us pray *(pause for silent prayer)*.
O God, our Creator and Redeemer,
Mary has given birth to the Savior
of our stricken humanity.
By his watchful protection
and her loving intercession,
shelter us from all evil
and secure our lives for the gospel,
now and for ever.
—Amen.

Psalm 48 Mary Is the New Jerusalem

Antiphon   O unutterable mystery! * The Virgin Mary
             is the city and the temple of God.

1. The LORD is great and worthy to be praised
    in the city of our God,

whose holy mountain rises in beauty,
the joy of all the earth.

2.   Mount Zion, true pole of the earth,
the Great King's city!
God, in the midst of its citadels,
is known to be its stronghold.

3.   For the kings assembled together,
together they advanced.
They saw; at once they were astounded;
dismayed, they fled in fear.

4.   A trembling seized them there,
like the pangs of birth.
By the east wind you have destroyed
the ships of Tarshish.

5.   As we have heard, so we have seen
in the city of our God,
in the city of the LORD of hosts
which God upholds forever.

6.   God we ponder your love
within your temple.
Your praise, O God, like your name
reaches the ends of the earth.

7.   With justice your right hand is filled.
Mount Zion rejoices;
the people of Judah rejoice
at the sight of your judgements.

8. Walk through Zion, walk all 'round it;
   count the number of its towers.
   Review all its ramparts,
   examine its castles,

9. that you may tell the next generation
   that such is our God,
   our God forever and ever.

Antiphon   O unutterable mystery! The Virgin Mary
            is the city and the temple of God.

Psalm Prayer

Let us pray *(pause for silent prayer).*
O Mother of God, shrine of the Holy Spirit,
all generations shall call you blest
and magnify God's name in honoring you.
Pray for the peace of the Church,
for spiritual safety inside its walls
and for the love of family and friends
in this world and in the life to come.
Blessed be God forever!
—Amen.

The Canticle of the Word
John 1:1-5, 10-12, 14

Antiphon   The Word of God became human *
            that we might become divine, alleluia!

Or this Antiphon

> The Ruler of the stars, *
> nurses at his Mother's breast, alleluia!

1. In the beginning was the Word,
   and the Word was with God,
   and the Word was God.
   He was in the beginning with God.
   All things came into being through him,
   and without him not one thing came into being.

2. What has come into being in him was life,
   and the life was the light of all people.
   The light shines in the darkness,
   and the darkness did not overcome it.

3. He was in the world,
   and the world came into being through him;
   yet the world did not know him.
   He came to what was his own,
   and his own people did not accept him.
   But to all who received him,
   who believed in his name,
   he gave power to become children of God.

4. And the Word became flesh
   and lived among us,
   and we have seen his glory,
   the glory of the Father's only Son,
   full of grace and truth.

5. Glory to the Father, and to the Son,
   and to the Holy Spirit:

6. as it was in the beginning, is now,
   and will be for ever. Amen.

One of the above antiphons is repeated.

Reading: Christ, the Exact Counterpart of God
Hebrews 1:1-4

Long ago God spoke to our ancestors in many and
various ways by the prophets, but in these last days he has
spoken to us by a Son, whom he appointed heir of all
things, through whom he also created the worlds. He is
the reflection of God's glory and the exact imprint of
God's very being, and he sustains all things by his
powerful word. When he had made purification for sins,
he sat down at the right hand of the Majesty on high,
having become as much superior to angels as the name
he has inherited is more excellent than theirs.

Pause for meditation.

Response

His mother treasured all these things in her heart,
alleluia!
—Her memory is glorious in heaven and on earth,
alleluia!

Canticle of the Blessed Virgin Mary
Luke 1:46-55

Antiphon   In the womb of the Mother *
resides the wisdom of the Father.

Or this Antiphon

O Savior of the world, * out of all creation
you selected servants to reveal your
    mysteries:
From among the angels, Gabriel;
From the human race, the Virgin Mary;
From the heavens, a star;
From the waters, the River Jordan,
to wash away the sins of the world, alleluia!

1. O praise, + my soul, the Lord!
   O glorify his name!
   In him my spirit thrills with joy,
   My Savior and my God!

2. From heaven he gazed on me,
   His lowly servant-maid;
   Behold, all ages yet to come
   Shall call me blest of God!

3. The Lord of wondrous power
   Has done great things for me;
   For ever blessed be his name
   Who is the holy One!

4. His mercy he reveals,
   To those who fear his name;
   From age to age his steadfast love
   Shall endlessly endure.

5. His arm is strong to save!
   He scatters all the proud;
   He casts the mighty from their thrones;
   He raises up the meek.

6. He fills the hungry poor
   With blessings from above;
   The rich he strips of wealth and power
   And empty sends away.

7. His mighty hand has grasped
   The hand of Israel,
   His servant-son, beloved by him
   With never-failing love.

8. Now is his promise kept,
   Once made to Abraham,
   That in his seed we would be blest
   For all eternity.

9. O Father, fount of joy,
   Your glory I adore!
   O loving Spirit, praise be yours,
   Who gave me God the Son! Amen.

Text: *Magnificat*, para. by James Quinn, S.J.

One of the above antiphons is repeated.

Litany

By the wondrous birth in time of the timeless Son of God, let us pray to the Lord.

—Lord, have mercy.

By the humble nativity of the King of glory in the cave of Bethlehem, let us pray to the Lord.

—Lord, have mercy.

By the splendid manifestation of the King of the Jews to the shepherds and the magi, let us pray to the Lord.

—Lord, have mercy.

By the spotless baptism of the beloved Son of God by John in the River Jordan, let us pray to the Lord.

—Lord, have mercy.

By the revealing sign of water made wine at the marriage of Cana, let us pray to the Lord.

—Lord, have mercy.

By the presentation of Jesus in the temple and the prophecies of old Simeon and Anna, let us pray to the Lord.

—Lord, have mercy.

By the finding of Jesus in the temple as he sat in the midst of the teachers of the Law, listening to them and asking them questions, let us pray to the Lord.

—Lord have mercy.

By the intercession of the great Mother of God, Mary
most holy, and of the whole company of heaven, let us
pray to the Lord.
—Lord, have mercy.

Spontaneous prayer

Closing Prayer

Blessed are you, O Mary:
in you the prophecies are fulfilled
and the dark sayings of the seers explained:
Moses and the burning bush and the pillar of fire,
Jacob and the ladder ascending into heaven,
David and the ark of the covenant,
Ezekiel and the closed and sealed door.
Now in Christ's birth their words are made plain.
Glory to the Father who sent his only Son
to show himself to the world through you,
to free us from error and sin
and make your memory glorious in heaven and on
    earth.
Blessed be the name of Mary, Virgin and Mother!
—Amen.

Blessing

Through the prayers of his Blessed Mother,
may the Lord grant + us safety and peace.
—Amen.

A sign of peace may be exchanged.

$\mathcal{A}$SSUMPTIONTIDE

T his season of Assumptiontide is dedicated to the glorious mysteries of Mary's falling asleep in death (her dormition), her bodily assumption into heaven, and her coronation as queen of heaven and earth. We concentrate now on her present, final, and eternal mode of existence at the right hand of her risen and ascended Son and Savior. She is "the great sign appearing in heaven: a woman clothed with the sun, with the moon under her feet, and a crown of twelve stars on her head" (Revelation 12:1). She is the Mother of the Church and of each and every Christian. In her we see the fulfillment of God's plan for all of us.

Assumptiontide is the longest season of the Marian year and has two divisions: 1) after the season of Christmas, it extends from February 3 through Shrove Tuesday; 2) after the season of Easter, from the Monday after Pentecost to the Saturday before the first Sunday of Advent.

Morning Prayer in Assumptiontide

O God, + come to my assistance.
—O Lord, make haste to help me.
Hail, Mary, full of grace,
—The Lord is with you.
Blessed are you among women,
—And blessed is the fruit of your womb, Jesus.
Holy Mary, Mother of God, pray for us sinners,
—Now and at the hour of our death. Amen.

Hymn

1. Mary crowned with living light,
    Temple of the Lord,
    Place of peace and holiness,
    Shelter of the Word.

2. Mystery of sinless life
    In our fallen race,
    Free from shadow, you reflect
    Plenitude of grace.

3. Virgin-mother of our God,
    Lift us when we fall,
    Who were named upon the Cross
    Mother of us all.

4. Father, Son and Holy Ghost,
    Heaven sings your praise;

Mary magnifies your name
Through eternal days.
Amen.

Text: © Stanbrook Abbey Music, 1974

Morning Psalms of Praise

Pray the Psalm or Canticle assigned to the day of the week and then turn to the reading on page 95.

Sunday
Psalm 145a A Hymn of Praise

Antiphon   Blessed are you, O Virgin Mary! * You carried the creator of the world in your womb.

1. I will give you glory, O God my king,
   I will bless your name for ever.

2. I will bless you day after day
   and praise your name for ever.
   You are great, LORD, highly to be praised,
   your greatness cannot be measured.

3. Age to age shall proclaim your works,
   shall declare your mighty deeds,
   shall speak of your splendor and glory,
   tell the tale of your wonderful works.

4. They will speak of your terrible deeds,
   recount your greatness and might.

They will recall your abundant goodness;
age to age shall ring out your justice.

5. You are kind and full of compassion,
slow to anger, abounding in love.
How good you are, LORD, to all,
compassionate to all your creatures.

6. All your creatures shall thank you O LORD,
and your friends shall repeat their blessing.
They shall speak of the glory of your reign
and declare your might, O God,

7. to make known to all your mighty deeds
and the glorious splendor of your reign.
Yours is an everlasting kingdom;
your rule lasts from age to age.

Antiphon   Blessed are you, O Virgin Mary! You carried
the creator of the world in your womb.

Psalm Prayer

Let us pray *(pause for silent prayer)*.
Lord our God,
you have made the Virgin Mary
the model for all who welcome your word
and who put it into practice.
Open our hearts to receive it with joy
and by the power of your Spirit
grant that we also may become a dwelling place

in which your Word of salvation is fulfilled.
We ask this through Christ Jesus our Lord.
—Amen.

Book of Mary (Washington, DC: United States Catholic Conference, 1987).

Monday
Psalm 145b God Alone Is Faithful

Antiphon   Hail, holy Mother! * In your womb you
carried the Lord of the universe.

1. I will give you glory, O God my king,
    I will bless your name for ever.

2. You are faithful in all your words
    and loving in all your deeds.
    You support all those who are falling
    and raise up all who are bowed down.

3. The eyes of all creatures look to you
    and you give them their food in due season.
    You open wide your hand,
    grant the desires of all who live.

4. You are just in all your ways
    and loving in all your deeds.
    You are close to all who call you,
    who call on you from their hearts.

5. You grant the desires of those who fear you,
    you hear their cry and you save them.
    LORD, you protect all who love you;
    but the wicked you will utterly destroy.

6. Let me speak your praise, O LORD,
    let all peoples bless your holy name
    for ever, for ages unending.

Antiphon   Hail, holy Mother! In your womb you
            carried the Lord of the universe.

Psalm Prayer

Let us pray *(pause for silent prayer)*.
Eternal Father,
you have established in the Virgin Mary
the royal throne of your wisdom.
Enlighten the Church by the Word of life,
that we may walk in the splendor of truth
and come to full knowledge of your mystery of love.
We ask this through Christ our Lord.
—Amen.

Book of Mary (Washington, DC: United States Catholic Conference, 1987).

Tuesday
Psalm 147a A Song of Thanksgiving

Antiphon   Rejoice, great Mother of God! *
           You are worthy of all praise.

1. Sing praise to the LORD who is good;
    sing to our God who is loving:
    to God our praise is due.

2. The LORD builds up Jerusalem
    and brings back Israel's exiles,
    God heals the broken-hearted,
    and binds up all their wounds.
    God fixes the number of the stars;
    and calls each one by name.

3. Our Lord is great and almighty;
    God's wisdom can never be measured.
    The LORD raises the lowly;
    and humbles the wicked to the dust.
    O sing to the LORD, giving thanks;
    sing psalms to our God with the harp.

4. God covers the heavens with clouds,
    and prepares the rain for the earth;
    making mountains sprout with grass
    and with plants to serve our needs.
    God provides the beasts with their food
    and the young ravens when they cry.

5. God takes no delight in horses' power
   nor pleasure in warriors' strength.
   The LORD delights in those who revere him,
   in those who wait for his love.

Antiphon   Rejoice, great Mother of God!
            You are worthy of all praise.

Psalm Prayer

Let us pray *(pause for silent prayer)*.
Holy and merciful God,
you are pleased by the humble
and by means of the Spirit accomplish in them
the great wonders of salvation.
Look upon the innocence of the Virgin Mary,
and give us simple and generous hearts
that respond without hesitation
to every sign of your will.
We ask this through Christ our Lord.
—Amen.

Book of Mary (Washington, DC: United States Catholic Conference, 1987).

Wednesday
Canticle of Judith 13:18-20; 15:9 (TEV)

Antiphon The Lord has cast down * the mighty
from their thrones and has lifted up the
lowly.

1. The Most High God has blessed you
more than any woman on earth.
How worthy of praise is the Lord God
who created heaven and earth!
He guided you as you cut off the head
of our deadliest enemy.

2. Your trust in God will never be forgotten
by those who tell of God's power.
May God give you everlasting honor
for what you have done.
May he reward you with blessings
because you remained faithful to him.
And did not hesitate to risk your own life
to relieve the oppression of your people.

3. You are Jerusalem's crowning glory,
the heroine of Israel,
the pride and joy of our people.

Antiphon The Lord has cast down the mighty
from their thrones and has lifted up the
lowly.

Psalm Prayer

Let us pray *(pause for silent prayer).*
Loving Savior,
by the willing cooperation and heroic faith of Mary,
the valiant woman of the gospel,
you crushed the head of our ancient enemy
and set all things under your feet:
By her continuing role in our salvation,
make her the pride and joy of believers
and the crowning glory of your Church.
You live and reign for ever and ever.
—Amen.

Thursday
Psalm 148 Praise Our Creator

Antiphon   From this time forth, * all ages will call me
blessed.

1. Praise the LORD from the heavens,
    praise God in the heights.
    Praise God, all you angels,
    praise him, all you host.

2. Praise God, sun and moon,
    praise him, shining stars.
    Praise God, highest heavens
    and the waters above the heavens.

3. Let them praise the name of the LORD.
   The Lord commanded: they were made.
   God fixed them for ever,
   gave a law which shall not pass away.

4. Praise the LORD from the earth,
   sea creatures and all oceans,
   fire and hail, snow and mist,
   stormy winds that obey God's word;

5. all mountains and hills,
   all fruit trees and cedars,
   beasts, wild and tame,
   reptiles and birds on the wing;

6. all earth's nations and peoples,
   earth's leaders and rulers;
   young men and maidens,
   the old together with children.

7. Let them praise the name of the LORD
   who alone is exalted.
   The splendor of God's name
   reaches beyond heaven and earth.

8. God exalts the strength of the people,
   is the praise of all the saints,
   of the sons and daughters of Israel,
   of the people to whom he comes close.

Antiphon   From this time forth, all ages will call me
           blessed.

Psalm Prayer

Let us pray *(pause for silent prayer)*.
Gracious Creator and Savior,
in union with our Blessed Mother
who unceasingly proclaims your greatness,
we ask you for the gift of perpetual praise
that your splendor may be the glory
of those whom you have chosen.
We ask this through Christ our Lord.
—Amen.

Friday
Psalm 149 God Delights in Saving the People

Antiphon   Blest is the Virgin Mary * who stood by the
cross of Jesus and now reigns with him for
ever.

1.   Sing a new song to the LORD,
   sing praise in the assembly of the faithful.
   Let Israel rejoice in its Maker,
   let Zion's people exult in their king.
   Let them praise God's name with dancing
   and make music with timbrel and harp.

2.   For the LORD takes delight in his people,
   and crowns the poor with salvation.
   Let the faithful rejoice in their glory,
   shout for joy and take their rest.

Let the praise of God be on their lips
and a two-edged sword in their hand.

Antiphon   Blest is the Virgin Mary who stood by the
cross of Jesus and now reigns with him for
ever.

Psalm Prayer

Let us pray *(pause for silent prayer)*.
God of all consolation,
you permitted the sharp sword of separation
to pierce the immaculate heart of Mary.
By her loving intercession
reveal to us the secrets of the blessed Passion
of your only Son our Savior,
and bring us at last to the home-haven of heaven
through the same Christ our Lord.
—Amen.

Saturday
Psalm 150 Let All Creation Sing God's Praise

Antiphon   You exalted the Blessed Virgin Mary, O
Christ, * and crowned her queen of heaven,
alleluia!

1. Praise God in his holy place,
Sing praise in the mighty heavens.

Sing praise for God's powerful deeds,
praise God's surpassing greatness.

2. Sing praise with sound of trumpet,
Sing praise with lute and harp.
Sing praise with timbrel and dance,
Sing praise with strings and pipes.

3. Sing praise with resounding cymbals,
Sing praise with clashing of cymbals.
Let everything that lives and that breathes
give praise to the LORD. Alleluia!

Antiphon   You exalted the Blessed Virgin Mary, O
Christ, and crowned her queen of heaven,
alleluia!

Psalm Prayer

Let us pray *(pause for silent prayer)*.
Living and majestic God,
as we devote ourselves to your honor and glory,
may a harmonious chorus of human praise
blend with the sweet voice of Mary our Queen
and the resounding canticles of rejoicing saints,
now and always and for ever and ever.
—Amen.

Reading: Praise of Lady Wisdom
Sirach 24:1, 3-7. 11-12

Wisdom tells of her glory: "I came forth from the mouth of the Most High, and covered the earth like a mist. I dwelt in the highest heavens, and my throne was in a pillar of cloud. Alone I compassed the vault of heaven and traversed the depths of the abyss. Over waves of the sea, over all the earth, and over every people and nation I have held sway. Among all these I sought a resting place; in whose territory should I abide? ... In the beloved city he gave me a resting place, and in Jerusalem was my domain. I took root in an honored people, in the portion of the Lord, his heritage."

Pause for meditation.

Response

Blest is the womb that bore you, O Christ, alleluia!
—And blest the breasts that nursed you, alleluia!

Canticle of Zachary
Luke 1:68-79

Antiphon   Great Mother of God, Mary most holy, *
you are more worthy of honor than the
cherubim and far more glorious than the
seraphim!

1. Blest be + the God of Israel
   Who comes to set us free
   And raises up new hope for us:
   A Branch of David's tree.

2. So have the prophets long declared
   That with a mighty arm
   God would turn back our enemies
   And all who wish us harm.

3. With promised mercy will God still
   The covenant recall,
   The oath once sworn to Abraham
   From foes to save us all:

4. That we might worship without fear
   And offer lives of praise,
   In holiness and righteousness
   To serve God all our days.

5. My child, as prophet of the Lord,
   You will prepare the way,
   To tell God's people they are saved
   From sin's eternal sway.

6. Then shall God's mercy from on high
   Shine forth and never cease
   To drive away the gloom of death
   And lead us into peace.

Text adapted by Carl P. Daw, Jr. © Hope Publishing Company

Antiphon   Great Mother of God, Mary most holy,
           you are more worthy of honor than the
           cherubim and far more glorious than the
           seraphim!

The Divine Praises

Blessed be God.

—Blessed be his holy name.

Blessed be Jesus Christ, true God and true man.

—Blessed be the name of Jesus.

Blessed be his most sacred heart.

—Blessed be his most precious blood.

Blessed be Jesus in the most holy sacrament of the altar.

—Blessed be the Holy Spirit, the Paraclete.

Blessed be the great Mother of God, Mary most holy.

—Blessed be her holy and immaculate conception.

Blessed be her glorious assumption.

—Blessed be the name of Mary, virgin and mother.

Blessed be Saint Joseph, her most chaste spouse.

—Blessed be God in his angels and in his saints.

Spontaneous prayer

Closing Prayer

Gracious God and Father,
in Mary, the first-born of redemption,

you have given us a Mother most tender.
Open our hearts to the joy of the Spirit,
and grant that by imitating the Virgin
we too may learn to magnify you
through the great work accomplished
in Christ, your Son,
who lives and reigns with you and the Holy Spirit,
one God, for ever and ever.
—Amen.

Book of Mary (Washington, DC: United States Catholic Conference, 1987).

Blessing

May the Virgin Mother mild + bless us with her holy Child.
—Amen.

A Salutation to the Blessed Virgin Mary

Hail, O Lady,
holy Queen,
Mary, holy Mother of God:
you are the virgin made church
and the one chosen by the most holy Father in heaven
whom he consecrated
with his most holy beloved Son
and with the Holy Spirit the Paraclete,
in whom there was and is
all the fullness of grace and every good.
Hail, his Palace!
Hail, his Tabernacle!
Hail, his Home!
Hail, his Robe!
Hail, his Servant!
Hail, his Mother!
And, hail all you holy virtues
which through the grace and light of the Holy Spirit
are poured into the hearts of the faithful
so that from their faithless state
you may make them faithful to God.

St. Francis of Assisi (1181–1226), trans. Regis J. Armstrong, OFM, Cap. and Ignatius Brady, OFM.

Evening Prayer in Assumptiontide

O God, + come to my assistance.
—O Lord, make haste to help me.
Hail, Mary, full of grace,
—The Lord is with you.
Blessed are you among women,
—And blessed is the fruit of your womb, Jesus.
Holy Mary, Mother of God, pray for us sinners,
—Now and at the hour of our death. Amen.

Hymn

1. Praise to Mary, heaven's gate,
   Guiding star of Christians' way,
   Mother of our Lord and King,
   Light and hope to souls astray.

2. When you heard the call of God
   Choosing to fulfill his plan,
   By your perfect act of love
   Hope was born in Adam's clan.

3. Help us to amend our ways,
   Halt the devil's strong attack,
   Walk with us the narrow path,
   Beg for us the grace we lack.

4. Mary, show your motherhood,
   Bring your children's prayers to Christ,

Christ, your Son who ransomed us,
Who for us was sacrificed.

5. Virgin chosen, singly blest,
Ever faithful to God's call,
Guide us in this earthly life,
Guard us lest, deceived, we fall.

6. Mary, help us live our faith
So that we may see your Son,
Join our humble prayers to yours,
Till life's ceaseless war is won.

7. Praise the Father, praise the Son,
Praise the Holy Paraclete;
Offer all through Mary's hands,
Let her make our prayers complete. Amen.

Text: *Ave, maris stella,* 9th century Latin hymn, trans. F. Quinn, O.P. et al. alt.

Evening Psalms

Pray the Psalm or Canticle assigned to the day of the week and then turn to the reading on page 112.

Sunday Psalm 113
The Lord Stoops to the Humble

Antiphon   You are all fair, O Mary; *
there is no stain of sin in you, alleluia!

1. Praise, O servants of the LORD,
   praise the name of the LORD!
   May the name of the LORD be blessed
   both now and for evermore!
   From the rising of the sun to its setting
   praised be the name of the LORD!

2. High above all nations is the Lord,
   above the heavens God's glory.
   Who is like the LORD, our God,
   the one enthroned on high,
   who stoops from the heights to look down,
   to look down upon heaven and earth?

3. From the dust God lifts up the lowly,
   from the dungheap God raises the poor
   to set them in the company of rulers,
   yes, with the rulers of the people.
   To the childless wife God gives a home
   and gladdens her heart with children.

Antiphon   You are all fair, O Mary;
            there is no stain of sin in you, alleluia!

Psalm Prayer

Let us pray *(pause for silent prayer)*.
Immaculate Virgin,
the mighty arm of God
raised you up from your humble state
and with your free assent

made you the Mother of his only Son.
As we venerate your name,
here and in every place,
assist our prayers before the Almighty
and be the Mother of your many children.
Blessed be the name of Mary, Virgin and Mother!
—Amen.

Monday
Psalm 121 The Lord Is Mary's Guardian

Antiphon   The Creator of all things *
                    rested in your tabernacle.

1. I lift up my eyes to the mountains;
    from where shall come my help?
    My help shall come from the LORD
    who made heaven and earth.

2. May God never allow you to stumble!
    Let your guard not sleep.
    Behold, neither sleeping nor slumbering,
    Israel's guard.

3. The LORD is your guard and your shade;
    and stands at your right.
    By day the sun shall not smite you
    nor the moon in the night.

4. The LORD will guard you from evil,
    and will guard your soul.

The LORD will guard your going and coming
both now and for ever.

Antiphon   The Creator of all things *
                     rested in your tabernacle.

Psalm Prayer

Let us pray *(pause for silent prayer).*
Great Mother of God,
you are the shrine of the Holy Spirit
and the ark of God's covenant.
God secured your life for our sake
as he watches over us
and shelters us from evil,
now and for ever.
—Amen.

Tuesday
Psalm 122 Mary: God's City, God's House

Antiphon   Blessed is the Virgin Mary, *
                     worthy of all praise, alleluia!

1. I rejoiced when I heard them say:
    "Let us go to God's house."
    And now our feet are standing
    within your gates, O Jerusalem.

2. Jerusalem is built as a city
    strongly compact.

It is there that the tribes go up,
the tribes of the LORD.

3. For Israel's law it is,
there to praise the LORD'S name.
There were set the thrones of judgment
of the house of David.

4. For the peace of Jerusalem pray:
"Peace be to your homes!
May peace reign in your walls,
in your palaces, peace."

5. For the love of my family and friends
I say: "Peace upon you."
For the love of the house of the LORD
I will ask for your good.

Antiphon   Blessed is the Virgin Mary,
            worthy of all praise, alleluia!

Psalm Prayer

Let us pray *(pause for silent prayer)*.
Holy Mary,
God's city, God's house, God's joy,
where the city and the temple are one,
pray for the peace of the earthly city,
for the happiness of our homes,
and for the welfare of the Church Universal,
now and for ever.
—Amen.

Wednesday
A Marian Canticle

Antiphon   You are the glory of Jerusalem, *
        the heroine of Israel,
        the pride and joy of your people!

1. Your love, O Mary, fairest of women,
    is more enticing than wine,
    more fragrant than fine perfume.
    Your name is like precious ointment
    drawing us in your footsteps (Song of Songs 1:1-4).

2. Arise, O Virgin Mary, my love, my fair one,
    and come away!
    For now the winter is past,
    the rain is over and gone,
    the flowers appear on the earth;
    the time of singing has come,
    the cooing of doves is heard in our land
    (Song 2:10-11).

3. You are altogether beautiful, my love;
    there is no flaw in you.
    How beautiful you are, my love,
    how very beautiful! (Song 4:6-7).

4. Mary the Virgin is a garden enclosed,
    a garden enclosed, a fountain sealed;
    a garden fountain, a well of living water,
    and flowing streams from Lebanon (Song 4:12, 15).

5. The holy Mother of God arises like the dawn,
   fair as the moon, bright as the sun,
   terrible as an army set in battle array! (Song 6:10).

6. Set me as a seal upon your heart, O Mary,
   as a seal upon your arm;
   for your love is as strong as death,
   your devotion an undying flame;
   a fire no waters can quench,
   no floods can drown (Song 8:6-7).

Antiphon   You are the glory of Jerusalem,
            the heroine of Israel,
            the pride and joy of your people!

Psalm Prayer

Let us pray *(pause for silent prayer)*.
Holy Mary, Virgin of virgins,
God's great sign in the sky,
and the splendid boast of your people:
Be now our loving intercessor
before the Blessed Trinity,
where you live and reign
in heavenly glory,
now and for ever.
—Amen.

Thursday
Psalm 126 God's Liberating Power

Antiphon   Happy is Mary * who believed
that what God promised her
would come true, alleluia!

1.   When the LORD delivered Zion from bondage,
it seemed like a dream.
Then was our mouth filled with laughter,
on our lips there were songs.

2.   The heathens themselves said: "What marvels
the LORD worked for them!"
What marvels the LORD worked for us!
Indeed we were glad.

3.   Deliver us, O LORD, from our bondage
as streams in dry land.
Those who are sowing in tears
will sing when they reap.

4.   They go out, they go out, full of tears,
carrying seed for the sowing;
they come back, they come back, full of song,
carrying their sheaves.

Antiphon   Happy is Mary who believed
that what God promised her
would come true, alleluia!

Psalm Prayer

Let us pray *(pause for silent prayer)*.
Holy Mother of Christ,
you put your faith in the angelic message,
bore the Son of the Most High,
and remain a virgin for ever.
Intercede for us
so that we who have been redeemed
may ascend to the throne of glory
where you reign with your Son,
now and for ever.
—Amen.

Friday
Psalm 129 Mary's Sufferings

Antiphon   Come and see, * all you who pass by,
if there is any sorrow like my sorrow.

1. "They have pressed me hard from my youth,"
   this is Israel's song.
   "They have pressed me hard from my youth
   but they could never destroy me.

2. They plowed my back like plowmen,
   drawing long furrows.
   But the LORD who is just, has destroyed
   the yoke of the wicked."

3. Let them be shamed and routed,
    those who hate Zion!
    Let them be like grass on the roof
    that withers before it flowers,

4. with which no reapers fill their arms,
    no binders make their sheaves
    and those passing by will not say:
    "On you the LORD's blessing!"

5. "We bless you in the name of the LORD."

Antiphon   Come and see, all you who pass by,
           if there is any sorrow like my sorrow.

Psalm Prayer

Let us pray *(pause for silent prayer)*.
Mother of Sorrows,
when your Son was ignored
by those who would not listen,
and persecuted and derided
by those who heard his message only too well,
your heart was pierced through and through
by the sword of separation.
May we who contemplate his blessed Passion
come to share in your pains and sorrows
and find consolation in his five precious wounds,

the indelible signs of love made visible.
Blessed be our Lady of Compassion!
—Amen.

Saturday
Psalm 132:7-11, 13-14, 17-18 Jesus, Son of David

Antiphon   You shall be a crown of beauty, O Mary, *
      in the hand of the Lord,
      a royal diadem in the hand of your God,
      alleluia!

1. "Let us go to the place of God's dwelling;
    let us go to kneel at God's footstool."

2. Go up, LORD, to the place of your rest,
    you and the ark of your strength.
    Your priests shall be clothed with holiness;
    your faithful shall ring out their joy.
    For the sake of David your servant
    do not reject your Anointed.

3. The Lord swore an oath to David,
    and will not revoke that word:
    "A son, the fruit of your body,
    will I set upon your throne."

4. For the LORD has chosen Zion;
    has desired it for a dwelling:
    "This is my resting place for ever,
    here have I chosen to live."

5.   There David's stock will flower;
      I will prepare a lamp for my Anointed.
      I will cover his enemies with shame
      but on him my crown will shine.

Antiphon   You shall be a crown of beauty, O Mary,
             in the hand of the Lord,
                a royal diadem in the hand of your God,
                alleluia!

Psalm Prayer

Let us pray *(pause for silent prayer)*.
Almighty God,
you gave a humble virgin
the privilege of being the Mother of your Son
and crowned her with the glory of heaven.
May the prayers of the Virgin Mary
prepare us for his coming again,
and raise us up to eternal life;
through the same Christ our Lord.
—Amen.

Reading: Lady Wisdom's Beauty
Sirach 24:13-17

I grew tall like a cedar in Lebanon, and like a cypress on the heights of Hermon. I grew tall like a palm tree in

En-gedi, and like rosebushes in Jericho; like a fair olive tree in the field, and like a plane tree beside water I grew tall. Like cassia and camel's thorn I gave forth perfume, and like choice myrrh I spread my fragrance . . . like the odor of incense in the tent. Like a terebinth I spread out my branches, and my branches are glorious and graceful. Like the vine I bud forth delights, and my blossoms become glorious and abundant fruit.

Pause for silent meditation.

Response

Blessed are you among women, O Seat of Wisdom, alleluia!
—And blessed is the fruit of your womb, Jesus, alleluia!

Canticle of the Blessed Virgin Mary
Luke 1:46-55

Antiphon   We turn to you for protection, *
              holy Mother of God.
              Listen to our prayers
              and help us in our needs.
              Save us from every danger,
              glorious and blessed Virgin.

1.   My soul + proclaims the greatness of the Lord,
     my spirit rejoices in God my Savior,
     for you, Lord, have looked with favor on your lowly
        servant.

2. From this day all generations will call me blessed:
   you, the Almighty, have done great things for me
   and holy is your name.
   You have mercy on those who fear you,
   from generation to generation.

3. You have shown strength with your arm
   and scattered the proud in their conceit,
   casting down the mighty from their thrones
   and lifting up the lowly.
   You have filled the hungry with good things
   and sent the rich away empty.

4. You have come to the aid of your servant Israel,
   to remember the promise of mercy,
   the promise made to our forebears,
   to Abraham and his children for ever.

5. Glory to God: Abba, our dear Father, the Word
   divine,
   and the Spirit, our advocate and guide:

6. now and always and for ever and ever. Amen.

Text: *English Language Liturgical Consultation.*

Antiphon   We turn to you for protection,
            holy Mother of God.
            Listen to our prayers
            and help us in our needs.
            Save us from every danger,
            glorious and blessed Virgin.

Text: *A Book of Prayers* (Washington, DC: International Commission on English in the Liturgy, 1982).

A Litany of the Blessed Virgin

(see pages 299-308)

Spontaneous prayer

Closing Prayer

Almighty Father of our Lord Jesus Christ,
you have revealed the beauty of your power
by exalting the lowly virgin of Nazareth
and making her the mother of our Savior.
May the prayers of this woman clothed with the sun
bring Jesus to the waiting world
and fill the void of incompletion
with the presence of her child,
who lives and reigns with you and the Holy Spirit,
one God, for ever and ever.
—Amen.

Alternate Opening Prayer for March 25, *The Roman Missal.*

Or this Closing Prayer

Beloved Mother of God,
when you passed out of this world,
your Son Jesus himself came to meet you
with all his angels and saints

115

and brought you before the Father,
with all manner of music, melody and joy.
There he set you in great peace and endless rest
and crowned you as Queen of heaven,
as Lady of all the world,
and as Empress of hell.
Beloved Mother,
bless us and help us to do the Father's will,
comfort us in this life,
and turn all our sorrow into joy,
for the sake of your blessed Son Jesus,
who took flesh and blood of you,
for our sake and for our salvation,
and now lives and reigns
in the embrace of the Holy Trinity,
one God, for ever and ever.
—Amen.

Text: *The Book of Margery Kempe*, chap. 79, trans. Barry Windeatt.

Blessing

Through the Virgin Mother blest
may the Lord + grant us our rest.
—Amen.

A sign of peace may be exchanged.

$\mathcal{T}$HE SEASON OF LENT

In the reformed Roman liturgy, Lent is designed for two purposes: 1) to prepare catechumens for baptism during the Vigil of Easter; and 2) to ready the already baptized for a renewal of their baptismal vows during the same Vigil. But in popular devotion, Lent concentrates our hearts on the passion and death of our Savior and on the sorrows of his Blessed Mother. Liturgy and popular devotion do not contradict one another here, but complement one another.

The very center of our religion is the paschal mystery, not just the fact of the death and resurrection of our Lord, but the profound inner meaning of it for each one of us and for the whole world. The fact is that if we come to the liturgy of Lent, Holy Week, and Easter without a sustained meditation on the sufferings of Jesus and Mary, we are highly unlikely to value them properly. That is why we have devotions like the Way of the Cross, the Sorrowful Mysteries of the Rosary, and the Lent of Our Lady. The hymns, psalms, readings, and prayers of the Lenten office—repeated over and over again during Lent—will assist us powerfully to enter into the living personalities of Jesus and Mary and their passing over from life through death and back to life again, for us and our salvation.

Mary of the Passion is usually called Our Lady of Sorrows or Mother of Sorrows, but she is also known as Our Lady of Tears and Our Lady of Compassion or Pity. In art she is usually shown standing at the foot of the cross or holding her dead Son in her arms after the descent from the cross. A hymn like the famous *Stabat Mater* (13th century) and passionate works of art like the Pieta of Michelangelo (St. Peter's church, Rome) or the Pieta of Ivan Mestrovic (University of Notre Dame) help us penetrate the depths of her agony.

The season of Lent lasts from Ash Wednesday until the Paschal Triduum (Good Friday, Holy Saturday, and Easter Sunday). See the Table of Feasts, page 30, for the dates of Ash Wednesday.

Lent Morning Prayer

O God, + come to my assistance.

—O Lord, make haste to help me.

Hail, Mary, full of grace,

—The Lord is with you.

Blessed are you among women,

—And blessed is the fruit of your womb, Jesus.

Holy Mary, Mother of God, pray for us sinners,

—Now and at the hour of our death. Amen.

Hymn

1. The new Eve stands before the Tree;
   Her dying Son speaks words of love:
   He gives his Mother as our Queen
   On earth below, in heaven above.

2. The second Adam sleeps in death,
   His side is pierced, his heart unsealed;
   The grace-filled Church, his sinless Bride,
   In blood and water is revealed.

3. We thank you, Father, for the Church,
   Where Christ is King and Mary Queen,
   Where through your Spirit you unfold
   A world of glory yet unseen. Amen.

Text: See John 19:26-27, 34; Genesis 2:21-24; Ephesians 5:25-27, para.
James Quinn, S.J.

Pray one or more of the following three psalms.

Psalm 3
Mary Is Sure of God's Protection

Antiphon   God has cast down * the mighty from their
thrones and has lifted up the lowly.

1.   How many are my foes, O LORD!
How many are rising up against me!
How many are saying about me:
"No help will come from God."

2.   But you, LORD, are a shield about me,
my glory, who lift up my head.
I cry aloud to you, LORD.
You answer me from your holy mountain.

3.   I lie down to rest and I sleep.
I wake, for you uphold me.
I will not fear even thousands of people
who are ranged on every side against me.

4.   Arise, LORD; save me, my God,
O LORD of salvation, bless your people!

Antiphon   God has cast down the mighty from their
thrones and has lifted up the lowly.

Psalm Prayer

Let us pray *(pause for silent prayer)*.
Mother of Sorrows,

you shared with your crucified Son
the jeers of unbelievers standing near the cross.
Help us to be sure of God's protection
and know that human opposition counts for nothing
in the face of the victory that is yours.
You are blest through all generations.
—Amen.

The Canticle of Hannah
1 Samuel 2:1-10

Antiphon   The Lord commands death and life *
              and gives victory to his Anointed.

1. I acclaim the Lord's greatness,
   source of my strength.
   I devour my foe,
   I say to God with joy:
   "You saved my life.
   Only you are holy, Lord;
   there is none but you,
   no other rock like you."

2. God knows when deeds match words,
   so make no arrogant claims.
   The weapons of the strong are broken,
   the defenseless gain strength.
   The overfed now toil to eat,
   while the hungry have their fill.

3. The childless bear many children,
   but the fertile learn they are sterile.
   The Lord commands life and death,
   consigns to Sheol or raises up.

4. God deals out poverty and wealth,
   casts down and lifts up,
   raising the poor from squalor,
   the needy from the trash heap,
   to sit with the high and mighty,
   taking their places of honor.

5. God owns the universe
   and sets the earth within it.
   God walks with the faithful
   but silences the wicked in darkness;
   their power does not prevail.

6. God's enemies will be broken,
   heaven thunders against them.
   The Lord will judge the earth,
   and give power to the king,
   victory to the Anointed.

Antiphon   The Lord commands death and life
            and gives victory to his Anointed.

Psalm Prayer

Let us pray *(pause for silent prayer)*.
Blessed Virgin Mary,
with Hannah the mother of Samuel,
you acclaimed the greatness of the Lord
and rejoiced in the gift of a child
chosen to bear God's mission.
Be a mother to the poor and needy
and give them a place of honor
in the universe that God owns.
All ages will call you blest!
—Amen.

Psalm 138 Mary's Song of Deliverance

Antiphon   Though I walk * in the midst of affliction
you give me life.

1. I thank you, Lord, with all my heart,
    you have heard the words of my mouth.
    In the presence of the angels I will bless you.
    I will adore before your holy temple.

2. I thank you for your faithfulness and love
    which excel all we ever knew of you.
    On the day I called, you answered;
    you increased the strength of my soul.

3. All the rulers of the earth shall thank you
   when they hear the words of your mouth.
   They shall sing of the LORD's ways:
   "How great is the glory of the LORD!"

4. The LORD is high yet looks on the lowly
   and the haughty God knows from afar.
   Though I walk in the midst of affliction
   you give me life and frustrate my foes.

5. You stretch out your hand and save me,
   your hand will do all things for me.
   Your love, O LORD, is eternal,
   discard not the work of your hands.

6. Glory to the holy and undivided Trinity:

7. now and always and for ever and ever. Amen.

Antiphon Though I walk in the midst of affliction
          you give me life.

Reading: The Sword of Division
Luke 2:22-35

When the time came for their purification according to
the law of Moses, Mary and Joseph brought Jesus up to
Jerusalem to present him to the Lord. . . . Now there was
a man in Jerusalem whose name was Simeon; this man
was righteous and devout, looking forward to the
consolation of Israel, and the Holy Spirit rested on
him. . . . Then Simeon blessed them and said to his

mother Mary, "This child is destined for the falling and the rising of many in Israel, and to be a sign that will be opposed so that the inner thoughts of many will be revealed—and a sword will pierce your own soul too."

Pause for meditation.

Response

O Queen of martyrs, who stood by the cross of Jesus,
—Pray for us in our hour of need.

Canticle of Isaiah 66:10-14a
Our Nursing Mother

Antiphon   Happy are you who weep now; *
                  you will laugh!

1.   Rejoice with Jerusalem, and be glad for her
     all you who love her;
     rejoice with her in joy,
     all you who mourn over her,

2.   that you may nurse and be satisfied
     from her consoling breast;
     that you may drink deeply with delight
     from her glorious bosom.

3.   For thus says the LORD:
     I will extend prosperity to her like a river,
     and the wealth of the nations

> like an overflowing stream
> and you shall nurse and be carried on her arm,
> and dandled on her knees.

4. As a mother comforts her child,
   so will I comfort you;
   you shall be comforted in Jerusalem.
   You shall see, and your heart shall rejoice;
   your bodies shall flourish like the grass;
   and it shall be known
   that the hand of the LORD
   is with his servants.

5. Glory to God: Creator, Redeemer, and Sanctifier:

6. now and always and for ever and ever. Amen.

Antiphon   Happy are you who weep now;
               you will laugh!

Litany of the Seven Swords

Mother of the Man of Sorrows:
As we recall the prophecy of old Simeon,
—Pray for us.
As we recall your flight into Egypt,
—Pray for us.
As we recall your loss of the boy Jesus in the Temple,
—Pray for us.
As we recall your meeting on the way to Golgotha,

—Pray for us.

As we recall you standing at the foot of the Cross,

—Pray for us.

As we recall the descent from the Cross,

—Pray for us.

As we recall the burial of Jesus,

—Pray for us.

Spontaneous prayer

Closing Prayer

God of mercy and compassion,
whose Son Jesus was lifted high on the Cross
in order to draw the whole world to himself,
and whose Mother suffered the pangs of martyrdom
as she witnessed his cruel sufferings and death:
Prepare us for the joys of paradise,
by virtue of the precious blood of Jesus
and the tears of his blessed Mother.
We ask this through the same Christ our blessed Savior.

—Amen.

Blessing

May the glorious passion of our Lord Jesus Christ
and the tears of our Lady of Compassion
+ bring us to the joys of paradise.

—Amen.

Sunset on Golgotha

The sun fails—
Your face pales,
The sun fails—
Mother of Sorrows,
you weep for your Son.

Anon., 13th century

Lent Evening Prayer

O God, + come to my assistance.
—O Lord, make haste to help me.
Hail, Mary, full of grace,
—The Lord is with you.
Blessed are you among women,
—And blessed is the fruit of your womb, Jesus.
Holy Mary, Mother of God, pray for us sinners,
—Now and at the hour of our death. Amen.

Hymn

1. We praise you, Queen in glory,
   Above all saints you reign;
   We praise you, Nurse of Jesus,
   Of him who knew such pain.
   You made yourself his handmaid
   From manger to cruel death;
   O Mary, still befriend us
   As we breathe forth our dying breath.

2. When Adam and Eve were banished
   From the garden, and hope seemed dead,
   God sent your Son, O Woman,
   To crush the serpent's head.
   The sinless Adam gave us
   With John to new Eve's care;

O sinless Eve, protect us,
Spotless Virgin beyond compare.

Text: James Quinn, S.J.

Pray one or more of the following three psalms.

Psalm 124 Mary Praises God's Protection

Antiphon   Blessed are the pure of heart, *
            for they shall see God.

1. "If the LORD had not been on our side,"
   this is Israel's song.
   "If the Lord had not been on our side
   when they rose against us,
   they would have swallowed us alive
   when their anger was kindled.

2. Then would the waters have engulfed us,
   the torrent gone over us;
   over our head would have swept
   the raging waters."

3. Blessed be the LORD who did not give us
   a prey to their teeth!
   Our life, like a bird, has escaped
   from the snare of the fowler.

4. Indeed the snare has been broken
   and we have escaped.

Our help is in the name of the LORD,
who made heaven and earth.

Antiphon   Blessed are the pure of heart,
for they shall see God.

Psalm Prayer

Let us pray *(pause for silent prayer)*.
Sweet Mother of God,
like your dear Son himself
you were snared by the fowler for a time
but freed at last by God's protection.
Be our safety and deliverance
as we try to walk the straight and narrow path
that leads to our home-haven of heaven.
Blessed be the great Mother of God,
Mary most holy!
—Amen.

Psalm 125 Mary's Unshakable Trust

Antiphon   Blessed are the meek, *
for they will inherit the earth.

1. Those who put their trust in the LORD
are like Mount Zion, that cannot be shaken,
that stands for ever.

2. Jerusalem! The mountains surround her,
so the LORD surrounds his people
both now and for ever.

3. For the scepter of the wicked shall not rest
over the land of the just
for fear that the hands of the just
should turn to evil.

4. Do good, LORD, to those who are good,
to the upright of heart;
but the crooked and those who do evil,
drive them away!

5. On Israel, peace!

Antiphon   Blessed are the meek,
            for they will inherit the earth.

Psalm Prayer

Let us pray *(pause for silent prayer).*
Holy Mary, Mother of God,
by the foreseen merits of the Savior,
you were saved from all taint of sin
and kept an upright heart.
Embrace your people
who are called Christians
that they may stand solid and strong

with your continued support,
now and for ever.
—Amen.

The Beatitudes True Happiness
Matthew 5:3-10

Antiphon   Blessed are those who mourn *
    for they will be comforted.

1. Blessed are the poor in spirit,
    for theirs is the kingdom of heaven.
    Blessed are those who mourn, for they will be
      comforted.
    Blessed are the meek, for they will inherit the earth.
    Blessed are those who hunger and thirst for
      righteousness,
    for they will be filled.

2. Blessed are the merciful, for they will receive
      mercy.
    Blessed are the pure in heart, for they will see God.
    Blessed are the peacemakers,
    for they will be called the children of God.
    Blessed are those who are persecuted for
      righteousness' sake
    for theirs is the kingdom of heaven.

3. Glory to the Father, and to the Son,
    and to the Holy Spirit:

4. as it was in the beginning, is now,
    and will be for ever. Amen.

Antiphon   Blessed are those who mourn
            for they will be comforted.

Reading: Mary at the Cross
John 19:25-27

Standing near the cross of Jesus were his mother, and his mother's sister, Mary the wife of Clopas, and Mary Magdalene. When Jesus saw his mother and the disciple whom he loved standing beside her, he said to his mother, "Woman, here is your son." Then he said to the disciple, "Here is your mother." And from that hour, the disciple took her into his own home.

Pause for meditation.

Response

The Roman lance pierced the heart of our Savior
—And the soul of his sorrowful Mother.

The Canticle of the Blessed Virgin Mary
Luke 1:46-55

Antiphon   Mary's canticle * puts an end
            to the lamentations of Eve.

1. My soul + gives glory to the Lord,
   In God my Savior I rejoice,
   My lowliness God did regard,
   Exalting me by his own choice.

2. From this day all shall call me blest,
   For God has done great things for me,
   Of all great names God's is the best,
   For it is holy; strong and free.

3. God's mercy goes to all who fear
   From age to age and to all parts.
   God's arm of strength to all is near;
   God scatters those who have proud hearts.

4. God casts the mighty from their thrones
   And raises those of low degree;
   God feeds the hungry as his own,
   The rich depart in poverty.

5. God raised his servant Israel,
   Remembering eternal grace,
   As from of old God did foretell
   To Abraham and all his race.

6. O Father, Son and Spirit blest,
   In threefold Name are you adored,
   To you be ev'ry prayer addrest,
   From age to age the only Lord.

Text: *Magnificat*, trans. J.T. Mueller, 1940, alt.

Antiphon   Mary's canticle puts an end
                 to the lamentations of Eve.

A Litany of the Blessed Virgin

(see pages 299-308)

Closing Prayer

Merciful God,
as Mary stood near the Cross,
Jesus gave her to us as our loving Mother.
By the power of her prayers,
make us glad to share the sufferings of her Son
and fill us with joy when he comes in glory
to judge the living and the dead.
We ask this through the same Christ our Lord.
—Amen.

Blessing

May the glorious passion of our Lord Jesus Christ
and the tears of our Sorrowful Mother Mary
+ bring us to the joys of paradise.
—Amen.

A sign of peace may be exchanged.

THE SEASON OF EASTER

As St. Augustine said: "We are Easter people and Alleluia is our song!" John's Gospel tells us that Mary was present at the foot of the Cross (John 19:25), and St. Luke tells us that she was present in the upper room after the Ascension (Acts 1:14). It seems inconceivable, therefore, that she was not with the other three Marys who saw the risen Christ on Easter Sunday; she was the first person to belong to the select group of believers in the person and mission of Jesus (Luke 1 and 2). She stayed with him on Golgotha when most of his disciples had fled; she and the other faithful women welcomed him back to life on Easter; she was the center of the nascent Church after the Ascension and at Pentecost.

After her death her glorious Assumption marks her as the first-fruits of the Resurrection, and her Coronation as Queen of Heaven reveals her as the undying intercessor for her beloved sons and daughters on earth.

The *Regina Coeli*, used as the antiphon for Mary's Canticle at Evening Prayer and in place of the threefold daily Angelus throughout the season of Easter, is a poetic summary of Mary's continuing role in the history of our salvation.

Easter Morning Prayer

O God, + come to my assistance.
—O Lord, make haste to help me.
Hail, Mary, full of grace,
—The Lord is with you.
Blessed are you among women,
—And blessed is the fruit of your womb, Jesus.
Holy Mary, Mother of God, pray for us sinners,
—Now and at the hour of our death. Amen.

Hymn

1. Easter glory fills the sky!
   Christ now lives, no more to die!
   Darkness has been put to flight
   By the living Lord of might.

2. See the stone is rolled away
   From the tomb where once he lay!
   He has risen as he said,
   Glorious Firstborn from the dead!

3. Mary, Mother, greet your Son,
   Radiant from his triumph won!
   By his cross you shared his pain,
   So for ever share his reign!

4. Christ, the Victor over death,
   Breathes on us the Spirit's breath!

Paradise is our reward,
Endless Easter with our Lord!

Text: James Quinn, S.J., *Praise for All Seasons.*

Pray one or more of the following three psalms.

Psalm 47 Acclaim the Risen Christ

Antiphon   Rejoice and be glad, * O Virgin Mary, alleluia!
for the Lord has truly risen, alleluia!

1. All peoples, clap your hands,
   cry to God with shouts of joy!
   For the LORD, the Most High, we must fear,
   great king over all the earth.

2. God subdues peoples under us
   and nations under our feet.
   Our inheritance, our glory, is from God,
   given to Jacob out of love.

3. God goes up with shouts of joy;
   the Lord goes up with trumpet blast.
   Sing praise to God, sing praise,
   sing praise to our king, sing praise.

4. God is king of all the earth,
   sing praise with all your skill.
   God is king over the nations;
   God reigns enthroned in holiness.

5.   The leaders of the people are assembled
with the people of Abraham's God.
The rulers of the earth belong to God,
to God who reigns over all.

Antiphon   Rejoice and be glad, O Virgin Mary, alleluia!
for the Lord has truly risen, alleluia!

Psalm Prayer

Let us pray *(pause for silent prayer)*.
Lord of life and death,
seated at the right hand of the Father,
put all the powers on earth under your feet
and by the intercession of your glorious Mother,
help us to sing with joy before your throne,
where you live and reign now and for ever.
—Amen.

Canticle of Isaiah 61:10–62:3
The Lord Delights in Mary

Antiphon   You shall be a royal crown * in God's hand,
O Mary, a bride adorned with her jewels,
alleluia!

1.   I will greatly rejoice in the LORD,
my whole being shall exult in my God;
for he has clothed me with the garments of salvation,

as a bridegroom decks himself with a garland,
and as a bride adorns herself with her jewels.

2. For as the earth brings forth its shoots,
and as a garden causes what is sown in it to spring up,
so the LORD God will cause righteousness and praise
to spring up before all the nations.

3. For Zion's sake I will not keep silent,
and for Jerusalem's sake I will not rest,
until her vindication shines out like the dawn,
and her salvation like a burning torch.

4. The nations shall see your vindication,
and all the kings your glory;
and you shall be called by a new name
that the mouth of the LORD will give.
You shall be a crown of beauty in the hand of the
    LORD,
and a royal diadem in the hand of your God.

Antiphon   You shall be a royal crown in God's hand,
            O Mary, a bride adorned with her jewels,
            alleluia!

Prayer

Let us pray *(pause for silent prayer)*.
Mary, beloved of God,
your Son's victory over death and hell

shines like the sun, blazes out like a torch.
May the world see your deliverance
and acknowledge you as earth's crown
for the Lord delights in you,
dressed in robes of justice and victory.
Blessed is the name of Mary, Virgin and Mother!
—Amen.

Psalm 46 Christ Is With Us

Antiphon   The LORD of hosts is with us; * alleluia!
                the risen Christ is our stronghold, alleluia!

1. God is for us a refuge and strength,
   a helper close at hand, in time of distress,
   so we shall not fear though the earth should rock,
   though the mountains fall into the depths of the sea;
   even though its waters rage and foam,
   even though the mountains be shaken by its waves.

2. The waters of a river give joy to God's city,
   the holy place where the Most High dwells.
   God is within, it cannot be shaken;
   God will help it at the dawning of the day.
   Nations are in tumult, kingdoms are shaken;
   God's voice roars forth, the earth shrinks away.

3. Come, consider the works of the LORD,
   the redoubtable deeds God has done on earth:
   putting an end to wars across the earth;

> breaking the bow, snapping the spear;
> burning the shields with fire.

4. "Be still and know that I am God,
   supreme among the nations,
   supreme on earth!"

Antiphon The LORD of hosts is with us; alleluia!
                the risen Christ is our stronghold, alleluia!

Reading: Eve and Mary
Genesis 3:13-15

The LORD God said to the woman, "What is this that you have done?" The woman said, "The serpent tricked me and I ate." The LORD God said to the serpent, "Because you have done this, cursed are you among all animals and among all wild creatures; upon your belly you shall go, and dust you shall eat all the days of your life. I will put enmity between you and the woman, and between your offspring and hers; he will strike your head, and you will strike his heel."

Pause for meditation.

Response

Mother of God, you are the mystical paradise, alleluia!
—That brought forth the precious tree of the cross, alleluia!

The Canticle of Zachary
Luke 1:67-79

Antiphon   Happy are you, O Virgin Mary, *
  and worthy of all praise, alleluia!
  for from you arose the Sun of
  Righteousness
  with healing in his wings, alleluia!

1. Blest be the Lord, + the God of Israel,
   Who brings the dawn and darkest night dispels,
   Who raises up a mighty Savior from the earth,
   Of David's line, a son of royal birth.

2. The prophets tell a story just begun
   Of vanquished foe and glorious vict'ry won,
   Of promise made to all who keep the law as guide:
   God's faithful love and mercy will abide.

3. This is the oath once sworn to Abraham:
   All shall be free to dwell upon the land,
   Free now to praise, unharmed by the oppressor's rod,
   Holy and righteous in the sight of God.

4. And you, my child, this day you shall be called
   The promised one, the prophet of our God,
   For you will go before the Lord to clear the way,
   And shepherd all into the light of day.

5. The tender love God promised from our birth
   Is soon to dawn upon this shadowed earth,

To shine on those whose sorrows seem to never
  cease,
To guide our feet into the path of peace.

Text: Owen Alstott, 1991 © Oregon Catholic Press.

Antiphon   Happy are you, O Virgin Mary,
            and worthy of all praise, alleluia!
            for from you arose the Sun of
            Righteousness
            with healing in his wings, alleluia!

A Litany of the Blessed Virgin Mary

Holy Mary, whose Son ascended the Cross for our sake,
—Pray for us.
Holy Mary, whose Son died on the Cross for us,
—Pray for us.
Holy Mary, whose Son lay dead and buried in the tomb
for us,
—Pray for us.
Holy Mary, whose Son descended among the dead to
deliver them,
—Pray for us.
Holy Mary, whose Son rose victorious from the grave
for our sake,
—Pray for us.
Holy Mary, whose Son ascended to the right hand of
the Father,

—Pray for us.

Holy Mary, whose Son created you a shrine of the Holy Spirit,

—Pray for us.

Holy Mary, whose Son assumed you body and soul into heaven,

—Pray for us.

Holy Mary, whose Son will come again in glory to judge the living and the dead,

—Pray for us.

Spontaneous prayer

Closing Prayer

Great and rescuing God,
by the resurrection of your Son,
our Lord Jesus Christ,
you gave joy to the world.
Grant that by the prayers of his Mother,
the Blessed Virgin Mary,
we may obtain the happiness of everlasting life;
through the same Christ our Lord.

—Amen.

Blessing

Christ has risen, alleluia!

—He has risen indeed, alleluia!

May the Virgin Mary mild
+ bless us with her holy Child.
—Amen.

Easter

Earth breaks up, time drops away,
In flows heaven, with its new day
Of endless life, when He who trod,
Very man and very God,
This earth in weakness, shame and pain,
Dying the death whose signs remain
Up yonder on the accursed tree—
Shall come again, nor more to be
Of captivity the thrall,
But the one God, All in all,
King of kings and Lord of lords,
As his servant John received the words,
"I died, and live forevermore!"

Robert Browning (1812–1889).

Easter Evening Prayer

O God, + come to my assistance.

—O Lord, make haste to help me.

Hail, Mary, full of grace,

—The Lord is with you.

Blessed are you among women,

—And blessed is the fruit of your womb, Jesus.

Holy Mary, Mother of God, pray for us sinners,

—Now and at the hour of our death. Amen.

Hymn

1. Mary the dawn, Christ the perfect Day.
   Mary the gate, Christ the heavenly Way.

2. Mary the root, Christ the mystic Vine.
   Mary the grape, Christ the sacred Wine.

3. Mary the wheat, Christ the living Bread.
   Mary the rose-bush, Christ the Rose blood-red.

4. Mary the font, Christ the cleansing Flood.
   Mary the chalice, Christ the saving Blood.

5. Mary the temple, Christ the temple's Lord.
   Mary the shrine, Christ the God adored.

6. Mary the beacon, Christ the haven's Rest.
   Mary the mirror, Christ the Vision blest.

7. Mary the mother, Christ the mother's Son,
   By all things blest while endless ages run.

Text: *Maria aurora*, trans. Paul Cross, 1949, alt.

Pray one or more of the following three psalms.

Psalm 23 The Good Shepherd

Antiphon   Rejoice and be glad, O Virgin Mary, *
               for your Son has truly risen, alleluia!

1.   LORD, you are my shepherd;
    there is nothing I shall want.
    Fresh and green are the pastures
    where you give me repose.
    Near restful waters you lead me,
    to revive my drooping spirit.

2.   You guide me along the right path;
    you are true to your name.
    If I should walk in the valley of darkness
    no evil would I fear.
    You are there with your crook and your staff;
    with these you give me comfort.

3.   You have prepared a banquet for me
    in the sight of my foes.
    My head you have anointed with oil;
    my cup is overflowing.

4.   Surely goodness and kindness shall follow me
    all the days of my life.
    In the LORD's own house shall I dwell
    for ever and ever.

Antiphon   Rejoice and be glad, O Virgin Mary, *
            for your Son has truly risen, alleluia!

Psalm Prayer

Let us pray *(pause for silent prayer).*
Good Shepherd of the flock,
when we walk through death's dark valley,
you are our guide and our shepherd.
As we share the eucharistic meal
each Day of the Lord,
fill us with the grace of your resurrection
and bring us in safety to your eternal presence
in the company of Mary and all the saints.
Blessed be the name of Jesus, now and for ever!
—Amen.

Psalm 113
Praise the Risen Lord

Antiphon   He is risen, alleluia! * He is not here,
            alleluia!

1. Praise, O servants of the LORD,
    praise the name of the LORD!
    May the name of the Lord be blessed
    both now and for evermore!
    From the rising of the sun to its setting
    praised be the name of the LORD!

2. High above all nations is the Lord,
   above the heavens God's glory.
   Who is like the LORD, our God,
   the one enthroned on high,
   who stoops from the heights to look down,
   to look down upon heaven and earth?

3. From the dust God lifts up the lowly,
   from the dungheap God raises the poor
   to set them in the company of rulers,
   yes, with the rulers of the people.
   To the childless wife God gives a home
   and gladdens her heart with children.

Antiphon   He is risen, alleluia! He is not here, alleluia!

Psalm Prayer

Let us pray *(pause for silent prayer)*.
Invincible Mother of God,
with you and all God's servants
in heaven and on earth,
we glorify our victorious and risen Lord
from the rising of the sun to its setting.
May he lift the lowly from the dust
and gladden mother Church with new children;
for his own name's sake.
—Amen.

Easter Anthem Christ Our Passover
1 Cor 5:7-8; Rom 6:9-11; 1 Cor 15:20-22

Antiphon   This is the Day the Lord has made, alleluia! *
               let us rejoice and be glad, alleluia!

1.   Christ our Passover has been sacrificed for us,
       therefore let us keep the feast,
       Not with the old leaven, the leaven of malice and
           evil,
       but with the unleavened bread of sincerity and
           truth. Alleluia!

2.   Christ being raised from the dead will never die
           again;
       death no longer has dominion over him.
       The death that he died, he died to sin, once for all;
       but the life he lives, he lives to God.
       So also consider yourselves dead to sin,
       and alive to God in Jesus Christ our Lord. Alleluia!

3.   Christ has been raised from the dead,
       the first fruits of those who have fallen asleep.
       For since by a man came death,
       by a man has come also the resurrection of the dead.
       For as in Adam all die,
       so also in Christ shall all be made alive. Alleluia!

4.   Glory to the Father, and to the Son,
       and to the Holy Spirit:

5.   as it was in the beginning, is now,
       and will be for ever. Amen.

Book of Common Prayer (1979).

Antiphon   This is the Day the Lord has made, alleluia!
let us rejoice and be glad, alleluia!

Reading: New Life in Christ
Romans 6:3-5

Do you not know that all of us who have been baptized into Christ Jesus were baptized into his death? Therefore we have been buried with him by baptism into death, so that, just as Christ was raised from the dead by the glory of the Father, so we too might walk in newness of life. For if we have been united with him in a death like his, we will certainly be united with him in a resurrection like his.

Pause for meditation.

Response

Blessed is Mary who believed, alleluia!
—That all God said to her would be fulfilled, alleluia!

The Canticle of the Blessed Virgin Mary
Luke 1:46-55

Antiphon   Rejoice, O Queen of heaven, alleluia! *
For the Son you bore, alleluia!
Has arisen as he promised, alleluia!
Pray for us to God the Father, alleluia!

1. My soul proclaims the Lord my God.
   My spirit sings God's praise;
   Who looks on me and lifts me up,
   That gladness fills my days.

2. All nations now will share my joy,
   For gifts of God outpoured.
   This lowly one has been made great.
   I magnify the Lord.

3. For those who fear the Holy One,
   God's mercy will not die.
   Whose strong right arm puts down the proud
   And lifts the lowly high.

4. God fills the hungry with good things,
   And sends the rich away.
   The promise made to Abraham
   Is filled to endless day.

5. Then let all nations praise our God,
   The Father and the Son,
   The Spirit blest who lives in us,
   While endless ages run. Amen.

Text: adapted from the text of Sr. Anne Carter, R.S.C.J.

Antiphon   Rejoice, O Queen of heaven, alleluia!
For the Son you bore, alleluia!
Has arisen as he promised, alleluia!
Pray for us to God the Father, alleluia!

A Litany of the Blessed Virgin Mary

(see pages 299-308)

Closing Prayer

God our Father,
you give joy to the world
by the resurrection of your Son,
our Lord Jesus Christ.
Through the prayers of his Mother, the Virgin Mary,
bring us to the happiness of eternal life.
We ask this through Christ our Lord.
—Amen.

Opening Prayer for the Common of the Blessed Virgin Mary, Easter
Season, *The Roman Missal.*

Blessing

Christ is risen, alleluia!
—He is risen indeed, alleluia!
May the King of glory, the Son of Mary,
+ bless us and keep us.
—Amen.

Nine

Marian

Feasts

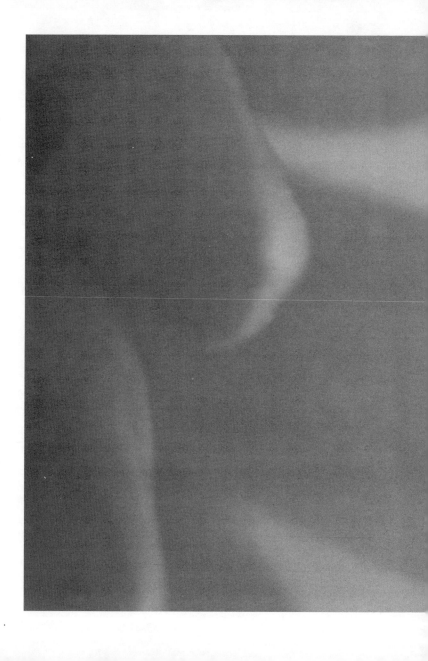

COMMON OF FEASTS
THROUGHOUT THE YEAR

Beside the great cycle of seasons and feasts of our Lord that composes the liturgical year, there is another overlapping cycle of feasts of our Lady.

The original feasts of this cycle sprang into being in the churches of the East as a result of the Council of Ephesus (431). This third ecumenical council vindicated the ancient Greek title of our Lady, *Theotokos* (*Deipara* in Latin; *God-bearer* or *Mother of God* in English) and occasioned an explosion of popular joy that brought into being feasts, processions, and pilgrimages in honor of the incarnation and Mary's role in it. The four feasts celebrated in the East were those of February 2 (the Meeting of Jesus and Simeon in the Temple), March 25 (the Annunciation), August 15 (the Dormition/Assumption), and September 8 (the Birthday of Mary).

In the Roman Church the original Marian feast was celebrated on the eighth day after Christmas in honor of her divine motherhood and perpetual virginity. By the late seventh century, popes of eastern origin had introduced the four eastern feasts of our Lady into the Roman liturgy and enhanced them with stational churches and popular processions in the city. As the Roman liturgy gradually replaced almost all the other Latin liturgies, these five feasts appeared everywhere in Europe and, after the sixteenth century, across the whole world of missionary endeavor.

Gradually and sporadically, fresh Marian feasts were added to local calendars and some of them were introduced into the general Roman calendar. The following nine feasts are representative of the Marian festivals celebrated in North America.

January 1	Solemnity of Mary, Mother of God
February 2	The Presentation/Purification
March 19	St. Joseph, Husband of Mary
March 25	The Annunciation
May 31	The Visitation

August 15   The Dormition/Assumption

September 8   The Nativity of Mary

December 8   The Immaculate Conception

December 12   Our Lady of Guadalupe

A Common of Feasts (Morning Prayer and Evening Prayer) follows. It provides a framework for the specific or proper additions to be inserted for each festival. The proper of the Nine Feasts (see pages 175-220) provides appropriate lessons for the Hour of Readings and proper readings, versicles, antiphons for the gospel canticles, and closing prayers for Morning and Evening Prayer.

When the Hour of Readings is used, the common office throughout the year (pages 223-244) provides appropriate psalms, hymns, and prayers. The lessons for the Hour of Readings in this section are inserted on page 239.

Morning Prayer
for the Common of Feasts

O God, + come to my assistance.

—O Lord, make haste to help me.

Hail, Mary, full of grace,

—The Lord is with you.

Blessed are you among women,

—And blessed is the fruit of your womb, Jesus.

Holy Mary, Mother of God, pray for us sinners,

—Now and at the hour of our death. Amen.

Hymn

1. The God whom earth and sea and sky
   Adore and praise and magnify,
   Whose might they claim, whose love they tell,
   In Mary's body came to dwell.

2. O Mother blest! the chosen shrine
   Wherein the Architect divine,
   Whose hand contains the earth and sky,
   Has come in human form to lie.

3. Blest in the message Gabriel brought;
   Blest in the work the Spirit wrought;
   Most blest, to bring to human birth
   The long desired of all the earth.

4. O Lord, the Virgin born, to you
   Eternal praise and laud are due,
   Whom with the Father we adore
   And Spirit blest for evermore. Amen.

Text: *Quem terra, pontus, sidera*, Venantius Fortunatus, ca. 530–609, trans. John M. Neale (1818–1866), alt.

A Marian Anthem

Antiphon   A great sign appeared in the sky: *
                    a woman clothed in the sun
                    with the moon under her feet
                    and a crown of twelve stars on her head,
                    alleluia! (Revelation 12:1)

1. Who is this coming forth like the rising dawn,
   fair as the moon, bright as the sun,
   terrible as an army set in battle array?
   —This is the great Mother of God, Mary most holy,
   who was conceived without original sin.

2. Who is this coming up from the desert
   like a column of incense smoke,
   breathing of myrrh and frankincense,
   and of every fine perfume?
   —This the great Mother of God, Mary most holy,
   who bore Christ whom the whole world cannot contain.

3. Who is this who ascends God's holy mountain

and stands in his sanctuary
with clean hands and a pure heart?
—This is the great Mother of God, Mary most holy,
who sits with Christ on his starry throne.

4. Who is this who washes her hands in innocence,
joins the procession about God's altar
and proclaims all his wonders?
—This is the great Mother of God, Mary most holy,
who alone, without peer, pleased our Lord Jesus
Christ.

5. Who is this exalted above the choirs of angels
and raised to the heavenly throne?
—This is the great Mother of God, Mary most holy,
who intercedes for us with our Lord Jesus Christ.

Antiphon   A great sign appeared in the sky:
a woman clothed in the sun
with the moon under her feet
and a crown of twelve stars on her head,
alleluia! (Revelation 12:1)

Prayer

Let us pray *(pause for silent prayer)*.
Great and glorious God,
you are wonderful in all your saints
and above all in the Mother of our Savior.
By the power of her prayers,
may we come to share in her holiness

and that of the whole company of heaven.
We ask this through Christ our Lord.
—Amen.

Reading from the Proper of the Feast

Canticle of Zachary
Luke 1:68-79

Antiphon from the Proper of the Feast

1. Blessed + are you, Lord, the God of Israel,
   you have come to your people and set them free.
   You have raised up for us a mighty Savior,
   born of the house of your servant David.

2. Through your holy prophets, you promised of old
   to save us from our enemies,
   from the hands of all who hate us,
   to show mercy to our forebears,
   and to remember your holy covenant.

3. This was the oath you swore to our father Abraham:
   to set us free from the hands of our enemies,
   free to worship you without fear,
   holy and righteous before you,
   all the days of our life.

4. And you, my child, shall be called the prophet of
   the Most High,

for you will go before the Lord to prepare the way,
to give God's people knowledge of salvation
by the forgiveness of their sins.

5. In the tender compassion of our God
   the dawn from on high shall break upon us,
   to shine on those who dwell in darkness and the
        shadow of death,
   and to guide our feet into the way of peace.

6. Glory to the Father, and to the Son,
   and to the Holy Spirit:

7. as it was in the beginning, is now,
   and will be for ever. Amen.

Text: *English Language Liturgical Consultation* (Nashville: Abingdon Press, 1988).

The proper antiphon is repeated.

Litany: Ave, Maria, Hail, Mary

Listen to me, Mother, listen to me, Mary,
kneeling I salute you:
—Ave, Maria.
The sky rejoices and the earth smiles
when the heart says:
—Ave, Maria.
Satan withdraws and all hell shudders
when the heart says:

—Ave, Maria.

The world seems small and the flesh trembles
when the heart says:

—Ave, Maria.

Sadness fades and happiness reigns
when the heart says:

—Ave, Maria.

Luke-warmness disappears and fervor returns
when the heart says:

—Ave, Maria.

Devotion grows and repentance is born
when the heart says:

—Ave, Maria.

Hope gushes forth and consolation increases
when the heart says:

—Ave, Maria.

The whole soul rekindles and love grows stronger
when the heart says:

—Ave, Maria.

Thomas á Kempis, *Discourse 25*, trans. Albin de Cigala (Westminster, MD: The Newman Press, 1956).

Pause for spontaneous prayer.

Closing Prayer of the Feast

Blessing

May the Blessed Virgin Mary + intercede for us with
the Lord.
—Amen.

Evening Prayer
for the Common of Feasts

O God, + come to my assistance.
—O Lord, make haste to help me.
You exalted your Mother, O Lord,
—And crowned her Queen of heaven.
Rejoice, O holy Mother of God,
—Lifted above the choirs of angels.
You are more worthy of honor than the cherubim
—And far more glorious than the seraphim.

Hymn

1. Hail, our Queen and Mother blest!
    Joy when all was sadness,
    life and hope you brought to earth,
    Mother of our gladness.

2. Children of the sinful Eve,
    sinless Eve, befriend us,
    exiled in this vale of tears:
    strength and comfort send us!

3. Pray for us, O Patroness,
    be our consolation!
    Lead us home to see your Son,
    Jesus, our salvation!

4. Gracious are you, full of grace,
    loving as none other,
    joy of heaven and joy of earth,
    Mary, God's own Mother!

Text: *Salve Regina*, eleventh century, trans. James Quinn, S.J.

Psalm 87 Mary Mothers Everyone

Antiphon   Blessed Lady, Mother of God, *
              in you all find their home, alleluia!

1. On the holy mountain is the city
    cherished by the LORD.
    The LORD prefers the gates of Zion
    to all Jacob's dwellings.
    Of you are told glorious things,
    O city of God!

2. "Babylon and Egypt I will count
    among those who know me;
    Philistia, Tyre, Ethiopia,
    these will be her children
    and Zion shall be called 'Mother'
    for all shall be her children."

3. It is God the Lord Most High
    who gives each a place.
    In the register of peoples God writes:
    "These are her children,"

and while they dance they will sing:
"In you all find their home."

Antiphon   Blessed Lady, Mother of God,
in you all find their home, alleluia!

Psalm Prayer

Let us pray *(pause for silent prayer)*.
Holy Mary,
help those in need,
give strength to the weak,
comfort the sorrowful,
pray for God's people,
assist the clergy,
intercede for religious.
May all who seek your help
experience your unfailing protection.
—Amen.

A Book of Prayers (Washington, D.C.: I.C.E.L., 1987).

Reading from the Proper of the Feast

The Song of the Virgin Mary
Luke 1:46-55

Antiphon from the Proper of the Feast

1. My soul + proclaims the greatness of the Lord,
   my spirit rejoices in God my Savior,
   for you, Lord, have looked with favor on your lowly
        servant.

2. From this day all generations will call me blessed:
   you, the Almighty, have done great things for me
   and holy is your name.
   You have mercy on those who fear you,
   from generation to generation.

3. You have shown strength with your arm
   and scattered the proud in their conceit,
   casting down the mighty from their thrones
   and lifting up the lowly.
   You have filled the hungry with good things
   and sent the rich away empty.

4. You have come to the aid of your servant Israel,
   to remember the promise of mercy,
   the promise made to our forebears,
   to Abraham and his children for ever.

5. Glory to the holy and undivided Trinity:
   now and always and for ever and ever. Amen.

Text: English Language Liturgical Consultation (Nashville: Abingdon Press, 1988).

The proper Antiphon of the feast is repeated.

Litany of the Blessed Virgin Mary (Akathist)

Hail, Mary! Hail, the restoration of the fallen Adam;
Hail, the redemption of the tears of Eve.
—Intercede for us with the Lord.

Hail, Mary! Height, hard to climb, for human minds;
Hail, depth, hard to explore, even for the eyes of angels.
—Intercede for us with the Lord.

Hail, Mary! Throne of wisdom;
Hail, security and hope for all who call upon you.
—Intercede for us with the Lord.

Hail, Mary! Heavenly ladder by which God came down
    to earth;
Hail, bridge leading from earth to heaven.
—Intercede for us with the Lord.

Hail, Mary! Favor of God to mortals;
Hail, access of mortals to God.
—Intercede for us to the Lord.

Hail, Mary! Mother of the Lamb and of the Good
    Shepherd;
Hail, fold for the sheep of his pasture.
—Intercede for us with the Lord.

Hail, Mary! Never silent voice of the apostles;
Hail, never conquered courage of champions.
—Intercede for us with the Lord.

Hail, Mary! Mother of the Star that never sets;
Hail, dawn of the mystic day.
—Intercede for us with the Lord.
Hail, Mary! Guide of the wisdom of the faithful;
Hail, joy of all generations.
—Intercede for us with the Lord.

Individual petitions are mentioned here.

Hail, Mary! Mother of God's own Son;
Hail, Mother of the Church.
—Intercede for us with the Lord.

Book of Mary (Washington, D.C.: I.C.E.L., 1987).

Closing Prayer from the Proper of the Feast

Blessing of the Feast

A sign of peace may be exchanged.

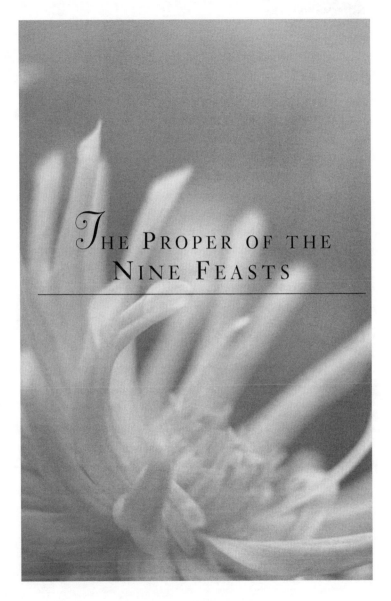

THE PROPER OF THE NINE FEASTS

January 1
Solemnity of Mary, Mother of God

On the eighth day after Christmas, the Roman liturgy celebrates its most ancient feast of Mary. In a special way this feast is a commemoration of her divine maternity and perpetual virginity. Mary trusted in God's word to her and so became the Mother of the God-Man and the Mother of his body, the church. In the Byzantine and Syrian Churches this memorial of the Mother of God is celebrated on December 26, and in the Coptic Church on January 6.

Lessons for the Hour of Readings

(insert in page 239)

1) Hebrews 2:9-17

2) From a Homily of St. John Chrysostom (ca. 347–407)

   Blessed Mary ever Virgin was indeed a great wonder. For what at any time has been or ever will be found more marvelous, more wonderful than she? She alone has surpassed heaven and earth in grandeur. Who more holy? No, not the Prophets, not the Apostles, not the Martyrs, not the Patriarchs, not the Angels, not the Thrones, not the Dominations, not the Cherubim, not the Seraphim nor any other living

176

creature visible or invisible; for no one can be found greater or more excellent than Mary. At the same time she is God's handmaid and his Mother; at the same time she is a virgin and a parent. She is the Mother of him who was begotten by the Father before every beginning, and whom Angels and humans acknowledge as Lord of all. Do you wish to know the pre-eminence this Virgin enjoys among the heavenly hosts? Covering their faces they are present in fear and trembling, but she offers humanity to him whom she brought forth, and through her we obtain forgiveness of sins.

Hail, then, O Mother, heaven, maiden, virgin, throne! You are the splendor, glory, and chief support of the Church! Unceasingly entreat Jesus, your Son and our Lord, for us that through you we may find mercy in the day of judgment and obtain those good things which are prepared for those who love God, through the favor and bounty of our Lord Jesus Christ; to whom with the Father and the Holy Spirit, be glory, honor and sovereignty, now and for all ages. Amen.

The Short Breviary (Collegeville, MN: The Liturgical Press, 1954).

Reading for Morning Prayer
Born of a Woman Galatians 4:4-7

When the fullness of time had come, God sent his Son, born of a woman, born under the law, in order to redeem those who were under the law, so that we might receive adoption as children. And because you are children, God has sent the Spirit of his Son into our hearts, crying, "Abba! Father!" So you are no longer a slave but a child, and if a child then also an heir, through God.

Response

The Word was made flesh, alleluia!
—And dwelt among us, alleluia!

Antiphon for the Canticle of Zachary

Rejoice, O great Mother of God, *
for the Sun of Righteousness has risen from your womb;
he gives light to those who walk in the shadow of death,
alleluia!

Text: Byzantine Troparion.

Reading for Evening Prayer
Full of Grace and Truth   John 1:14, 16-18

The Word became flesh and lived among us, and we have seen his glory, the glory as of a father's only son, full of grace and truth. . . . From his fullness we have all received, grace upon grace. The law indeed was given through Moses; grace and truth came through Jesus Christ. No one has ever seen God. It is God the only Son, who is close to the Father's heart, who has made him known.

Response

Blessed be the great Mother of God, Mary most holy, alleluia!
—She bore the Son of the eternal Father, alleluia!

Antiphon for the Canticle of Mary

Hail, holy Mother! * the child you bore
is the Lord of heaven and earth, alleluia!

Marian Litany

(see pages 299-308) followed by this Closing Prayer:

Father,
Source of light in every age,
the Virgin conceived and bore your Son
who is called Wonderful God, Prince of Peace.
May her prayer, the gift of a mother's love,
be your people's joy through all ages.
May her response, born of a humble heart,
draw your Spirit to rest on your people.

Grant this through Christ our Lord.
—Amen.

Alternate Opening Prayer for January 1, *The Roman Missal.*

Blessing

Through the prayers of the Virgin Mother,
may the Lord + grant us safety and peace.
—Amen.

February 2
The Presentation of the Lord

The Jerusalem Church was already celebrating the feast of the Presentation of Jesus in the Temple by the middle of the fourth century. Introduced at Rome in the seventh century, this feast of the Lord was called the "Feast of St. Simeon" or the "Meeting of Jesus and Simeon," and commemorated his prophetic reception by the aged Simeon and the widowed Anna the prophet (Luke 2:22-38). It marks a further entry of Jesus and his parents into the world of the Law and the Prophets, a coming marked out by both joy and future suffering. In earlier Latin calendars, February 2 was called the "Purification of the Blessed Virgin Mary" from a lesser legal aspect of the Temple visit. In England it was called "Ladyday" or "Candlemas" from the annual blessing of candles for church and home on this feast.

Lessons for the Hour of Readings

(insert in page 239)

1) Exodus 13:1-3a, 11-16

2) Purification and Presentation

Mary is purified, although she is the noblest flower and the purest glory of Israel. She humbly submits to the law of the Temple, empty as it is of the ark of the covenant, while she herself is the temple of the Holy Spirit, the ark of the new covenant. Jesus is redeemed according to the law of Moses, yet he himself is the redeemer, not only of Israel, but of the whole world. He is presented in the Temple, but he is greater than the Temple (Matthew 12:6); it is he who sanctifies the Temple and every offering that we can make to God.

Jesus is welcomed in the Temple by two representatives of the Poor of the House of Israel who were awaiting the comforter of their nation: Simeon and Anna the prophetess, two old people, for the former dispensation had grown old and was nearing the end of its life. Simeon too is a prophet. In a mysterious way he sees Jesus as destined to be "a sign that will be opposed" (Luke 2:34). Thus he foresees from afar the paschal drama which will replace the old Temple by the new. The whole of Israel's expectation is summed up in the persons of Simeon and Anna. In them Israel, through Simeon's prophecy, accepts the fact that she must give place to reality and be superseded by it [cf. Luke 2:29-32].

The prophetic theme of this first coming of Jesus to the Temple is already the same as that of the second, when he comes to purify the Temple. The first feature in the new reality Christ brings is the universal scope of salvation; God's house will be open to all nations. This universal significance of the Presentation completes the earlier meaning of the hidden coming of Christmas Day, when the angels and people of every condition acclaimed or acknowledged the Lord. The advent of Jesus and his first coming to the Temple take on a cosmic character. . . . They foreshadow the time when the whole creation will once more become the temple of God.

Yves Congar, O.P., *The Mystery of the Temple* (Westminster, MD: Newman Press, 1962).

Reading for Morning Prayer
The Messenger   Malachi 3:1-4 (TEV)

The Lord Almighty: "I will send my messenger to prepare the way for me. Then the Lord you are looking for will suddenly come to his Temple. The messenger you long to see will come and proclaim my covenant."

Response

You are a light of revelation to the Gentiles, alleluia!
—And the glory of your people Israel, alleluia!

Antiphon for the Canticle of Zachary

When Mary and Joseph * presented the child Jesus in the Temple, old Simeon took the child in his arms and praised God, alleluia!

Reading for Evening Prayer
Luke 2:27-38

Guided by the Spirit, Simeon came into the temple; and when the parents brought in the child Jesus, to do for him what was customary under the law, Simeon took him in his arms and praised God. . . . And the child's father and mother were amazed at what was being said about him. . . There was also a prophet, Anna the daughter of Phanuel. . . . At that moment she came [into the temple], and began to praise God and to speak about the child to all who were looking for the redemption of Jerusalem.

Response

My eyes have seen the salvation, alleluia!
—Which you prepared in the sight of every people, alleluia!

Antiphon for the Canticle of Mary

Old Simeon took the child in his arms, alleluia! *
but the child was old Simeon's Lord, alleluia!

Marian Litany

(see pages 299-308) followed by this Closing Prayer:

Almighty and everlasting God,
old Simeon and the prophet Anna
rejoiced at the coming of your Son into the Temple.
May we enter into their joy
and await your coming in glory at the end of time.
We ask this through Christ our Lord.
—Amen.

Blessing

By the prayers of the Blessed Virgin Mary
and of St. Joseph her spouse,
may the Light of the world + be our salvation.
—Amen.

March 19
St. Joseph, Husband of Mary

Although he is largely in the background of the gospel accounts, Saint Joseph was the head of the Holy Family, the legitimate husband of Mary and the foster father of Jesus. He is the patron of those who work with their hands, of the dying, and of the universal church. From the tenth century this feast was observed in many local calendars but only entered the Roman calendar in 1479; it was extended to the whole Latin Church in 1621.

Lessons for the Hour of Readings

(insert in page 239)

1) Hebrews 11:1-6

2) From a homily of St. Bernard of Clairvaux (1090–1153)

   From the great honor of being privileged to be called and considered the father of God (though, of course, he was only the foster father), we may judge the character and spirit of St. Joseph. Here we must not forget that great patriarch, Joseph, who in ancient days was sold into Egypt and of whom St. Joseph was heir not only in name, but in purity, innocence and grace. To the former was given the gift of knowing the mysteries of dreams; the latter was graced not only with knowledge of, but even participation in the mysteries of heaven. The former Joseph kept foodstuffs, not indeed for himself but for all the people, while the latter received into his care the living Bread from heaven for himself as well as for all the world. We dare not doubt that blessed Joseph, to whom the Mother of the Savior was espoused, was a good and faithful servant, for the Lord appointed him guardian and consoler of his Mother, nourisher of his own body, and coadjutor on earth in the incomprehensible designs of heaven.

The Short Breviary (Collegeville: The Liturgical Press, 1954).

Reading for Morning Prayer
Sirach 26:1-4

Happy is the husband of a good wife; the number of his days will be doubled. A loyal wife brings joy to her husband, and he will complete his years in peace. A good wife is a great blessing; she will be granted among the blessings of the man who fears the Lord. Whether rich or poor, his heart is content, and at all times his face is cheerful.

Response

Joseph was a man, alleluia!
—Who always did what was right, alleluia!

Antiphon for the Canticle of Zachary

Joseph was a faithful and wise steward
* whom the Lord set over his family.

Reading for Evening Prayer
Name Him Jesus   Matthew 1:18-21

When Jesus' mother Mary was engaged to Joseph, but before they lived together, she was found to be with child from the Holy Spirit. Her husband Joseph, being a righteous man and unwilling to expose her to public disgrace, planned to dismiss her quietly. But just when he had resolved to do this, an angel of the Lord appeared to him in a dream and said, "Joseph, son of David, do not be afraid to take Mary as your wife, for the child conceived in her is from the Holy Spirit. She will bear a son, and you are to name him Jesus, for he will save his people from their sins."

Response

Jesus was in the eyes of the Law, alleluia!
—The son of Joseph, alleluia!

Antiphon for the Canticle of Mary

The Lord has put * his faithful servant
in charge of his household, alleluia!

Litany of St. Joseph

(see pages 308-310) followed by this Closing Prayer:

O God our protector,
in your providence you chose Saint Joseph
as the husband of Mary and the father of Jesus.
May we who revere him as our guardian
have him as our intercessor in heaven.
We ask this through Christ our Lord.
—Amen.

Opening Prayer for March 19, *The Roman Missal.*

Blessing

As we celebrate the memory of Saint Joseph,
may Christ our Lord + bless us and keep us.
—Amen.

March 25
The Annunciation

Very early on, March 25 was considered the day on which Jesus was conceived at the message of an angel and also the day on which he died on the cross. In the East it became a public festival of the Incarnation in the fifth century and was brought to Rome in the seventh. Mary's "Yes" to the angelic message made her the highly favored daughter of God the Father, the mother of God the Son, and our model of willing obedience to the call of the Holy Spirit in our lives.

Lessons for the Hour of Readings

(insert in page 239)

1) 1 Chronicles 17:1-15

2) From a Homily of St. Proclus of Constantinople (434–446)

   He who was divinely generated by the Father before all ages, the Same is generated by a Virgin today, for our salvation's sake. There above, he is the only Son, generated according to divinity, by the only Father; here below he is God, but not just a man according to humanity. There above, he is with the Father in an inexpressible way; here below, he is born from his

Mother in an unspeakable way. There above, he has no mother; here below, he has no earthly father. Above, the firstborn, before all ages; below, the firstborn of a Virgin, according to the mystery of the incarnation.

Precisely for this reason, the Virgin is Mother of God (*Theotokos*). Thus, even after giving birth, she remained a virgin. The birth is inexplicable because of the inaccessible mystery, but the Word became visible through the event of his incarnation. Consider that he remained what he was and became what he was not, passable and impassible together, according to what was seen, remaining consubstantial with the Father according to his divinity and consubstantial with us according to his humanity, except in the matter of sin.

From Homily 5, 17 on the Nativity; *Le Museon* 54 (1941), trans. Thomas Buffer.

Reading for Morning Prayer
The Son of God   Luke 1:35-38

The angel said to Mary, "The Holy Spirit will come upon you, and the power of the Most High will overshadow you; therefore the child to be born will be holy; he will be called Son of God. . . . For nothing will be impossible with God." Then Mary said, "Here am I, the servant of

the Lord; let it be with me according to your word."
Then the angel departed from her.

Response

The Word was made flesh, alleluia!
—And lived among us, alleluia!

Antiphon for the Canticle of Zachary

God so loved the world * that he sent his only Son
in our mortal nature to save us, alleluia!

Reading for Evening Prayer
Eternal Life   1 John 1:1-2 (TEV)

We write to you about the Word of life, which has
existed from the very beginning. We have heard it, and
we have seen it with our eyes; yes, we have seen it, and
our hands have touched it. When this life became visible,
we saw it; so we speak of it and tell you about the eternal
life which was with the Father and was made known to us.

Response

The Holy Spirit will come upon you, Mary, alleluia!
—And the power of the Most High will overshadow
you, alleluia!

Antiphon for the Canticle of Mary

Today is the beginning of our salvation *
and the revelation of the eternal mystery:
the Son of God becomes the Son of the Virgin Mary
as Gabriel proclaims the good news of God's grace.
Rejoice, O Mary, full of grace, the Lord is with you!

Byzantine Troparion

Marian Litany

(see pages 299-312) followed by this Closing Prayer:

Pour forth, O Lord,
your grace into our hearts,
that we to whom the incarnation of Christ your Son
was made known by the message of an angel,
may by his passion and cross
be brought to the glory of his resurrection;
through the same Christ our Lord.
—Amen.

Blessing

May the Virgin Mary mild
+ bless us with her holy child.
—Amen.

May 31
The Visitation

As soon as Mary learned from the angel that Elizabeth her cousin had conceived a child in her old age, she "went in haste" to visit her. Mary visits Elizabeth, Jesus visits John in her womb and sanctifies him for his great mission as forerunner of the Messiah. Elizabeth greets Mary: "Blessed are you among women and blessed is the fruit of your womb," and John silently hails Jesus as the Savior. Then Mary sings her *Magnificat* that resounds down the ages in our daily office, reminding us that "God casts down the mighty from their thrones and lifts up the lowly."

This feast was begun by the Franciscans and was officially adopted in the General Chapter of the Order in 1263. Pope Urban VI introduced it into the Roman calendar in 1389 as one of his efforts at obtaining the end of the disastrous papal schism of the period. In the sixteenth century Pope Pius V (1566–1572) extended it to the whole Latin Church. In 1969 the feast was transferred from its old date of July 2 to May 31, a date more in keeping with the gospel narrative because it falls between the solemnity of the Annunciation (March 25) and the birthday of St. John the Baptist (June 24).

Lessons for the Hour of Readings

(insert in page 239)

1) Song of Songs 2:8-14; 8:6-7

2) Mary, the First Christian Revolutionary

The backdrop of the *Magnificat* [Mary's canticle] is the tragic character of a world that is unjustly ordered and therefore an obstacle to God's plan for society and human beings. However, God has resolved to intervene through the Messiah and to inaugurate new relationships with all things. All Israel, and all humanity, yearn for this saving moment. Mary has understood: Now, in her womb, suddenly the principle and agent of all salvation and liberation has sprung to human life. It is as if Jesus were already exclaiming, "This is the time of fulfillment. The Reign of God is at hand! Reform your lives and believe in the gospel!" (Mark 1:15)— and the cry he will one day utter as he starts enthusiastically down the highways and byways of Galilee.

Mary, too, is filled with jubilation and intones her hymn of laud and joy. Nor is her joy a kind of "whistling in the dark," fingers crossed, hoping but without a real basis for hope. No, Mary is filled with messianic exaltation. God has become the Savior (Luke 1:47) and has looked kindly on the lowly servant woman (Luke 1:48). And behold: Mary becomes the prototype of what God intends to do for all humanity. This is why she can sing that every generation will call her blessed (Luke 1:48).

God is Holy, and the Utterly Other, who dwells in inaccessible light (see Luke 1:49). But God does not live at a sovereign distance, far from the excruciating cries of the children of God. The Blessed Virgin can proclaim that God's mercy extends from age to age (Luke 1:50). God has left the resplendent shadows of an inaccessible abode and now draws near the murky light of the human race. God enters the conflict, takes up the cause of the conquered and the marginalized against the mighty. God strikes down those who "make history," a history that they themselves intend to write in books filled with their self-magnification.

The mercy of God is not reserved for the end time alone. The mercy of God will not allow the wound to fester. The mercy of God takes historical forms, is made concrete in deeds that transform the interplay of forces. The proud, with power in their hands, the wealthy, do not have the last word. They think they have, but the divine justice is already upon them, in history itself. They will be stripped of their power, the mask will be torn from their proud faces, and they will be sent away empty-handed (Luke 1:51-53). The Reign of God is anything but the consecration of this world's "law and order"—the decree of the overly ambitious. The Reign of God is precisely a protest against the "order" of this world. The Reign of Justice is the reign of a different justice. God promised this new world to our ancestors, and this promise is our certitude.

Leonardo Boff, O.F.M. in Andrew Harvey, *Teachings of the Christian Mystics* (Boston and London: Shambhala, 1998), pp. 175-177.

Reading for Morning Prayer
Come Away, My Love   Song of Songs 2:10-14

The lover calls: "Come with me, my love, come away. For the long wet months are past, the rains have fed the earth and left it bright with blossoms. Birds wing in the low sky, dove and songbird singing in the open air above, earth nourishing tree and vine, green fig and tender grape, green and tender fragrance. Come with me, my love, come away. My dove in the clefts of the rocks, the secret of steep ravines. Come, let me look at you. Let me hear you."

The Song of Songs, trans. Marcia Fallz (HarperSanFrancisco, 1993), #9-10.

Response

Blessed are you among women, alleluia!
—And blessed is the fruit of your womb, alleluia!

Antiphon for the Canticle of Zachary

When Elizabeth heard Mary's greeting, *
the baby moved within her, alleluia!

Reading for Evening Prayer
Blessed Are You   Luke 1:41-47

When Elizabeth heard Mary's greeting, the child leaped in her womb. And Elizabeth was filled with the Holy Spirit and exclaimed with a loud cry, "Blessed are you among women, and blessed is the fruit of your womb. And why has this happened to me, that the mother of my Lord comes to me? For as soon as I heard the sound of your greeting, the child in my womb leaped for joy. And blessed is she who believed that there would be a fulfillment of what was spoken to her by the Lord." And Mary said, "My soul magnifies the Lord, and my spirit rejoices in God my Savior."

Response

God has raised up a mighty Savior for us, alleluia!
—In the house of his servant David, alleluia!

Antiphon for the Canticle of Mary

The Lord has looked with favor on his lowly servant; *
all generations will call me blessed, alleluia!

Marian Litany

(see pages 299-312) followed by this Closing Prayer:

Overshadowing and moving God,
you inspired the Virgin Mary
to visit her cousin Elizabeth
and to sanctify the Baptist in her womb.
May the child-bearing of Mary,
the beginning of our salvation,
enlighten and inspire us
to love and serve our neighbor
and bring us an increase of peace.
We ask this through Christ our Lord.
—Amen.

Blessing

May the holy Child of the Blessed Virgin
+ sanctify and save us.
—Amen.

August 15
The Dormition and Assumption of Mary

This ancient feast of the falling asleep in death and of the bodily assumption of the Virgin Mary is observed on the dedication day of one of the first churches erected in her honor at Jerusalem (fifth century). It was introduced into the Roman liturgy around the middle of the seventh century. In Jerusalem, Rome, and Constantinople, great civic processions were held in her honor on this day, and in many countries it became a kind of early harvest festival when churches were strewn with herbs and flowers to mark the occasion. On November 1, 1950, Pope Pius XII defined this venerable article of faith as a dogma and provided the feast with new texts to enhance it.

Lessons for the Hour of Readings

(insert in page 239)

1) Ephesians 1:16–2:10

2) From a Homily of St. John of Damascus (ca. 675–ca. 749)

My dear brothers and sisters: To the temple of the Lord not made by hands there today has come to rest Mary, a holy tabernacle, re-enlivened by the living God. David, her forefather, rejoices, and with him choirs of Angels and Archangels; choirs of Virtues and Principalities are glorifying her; choirs of Powers and of Dominations and of Thrones sing exultingly to her; the Cherubim and the Seraphim praising chant her glory. For today the immaculate Virgin, undefiled by earthly affection, whose nourishment was heavenly thoughts, returns not again to the world with re-enlivened body, but is assumed into the tabernacles of heaven.

How could that one taste death from whom the true life flowed out to all? Yet she did fall under the law inflicted by him whom she bore, and as a daughter of the old Adam she suffered the old sentence of death, even as her Son who is life itself. But now as the Mother of the living God, she is fittingly taken up to heaven by him. For how could death feed on this truly blessed one who had eagerly listened to the word of God? who at the Archangel's salutation, filled with the Holy Spirit, conceived the Son of God? who without pain gave birth to him? whose whole being was ever consecrated to her Creator? Could hell receive such a one? Could corruption destroy a body in which Life had been brought forth? For her a way is prepared to heaven—a way that is straight and fair and easy. For if Christ, the way and the truth, has said: "Where I am there also shall my servant be," does it not follow that his Mother is surely with him?

The Short Breviary (Collegeville, MN: The Liturgical Press, 1954).

Morning and Evening Poem

If flowers are too stainless to remain
Concealed in the dark caverns of the earth,
But must be lifted up by God again
To know a second birth—a glad rebirth!
How could Christ leave her body in the tomb
Who was above all other women blest,
Who gave him refuge in her virgin womb,
And fed him on the lilies of her breast?
Is she not fairer far than any flower?
What bloom could ever boast her loveliness?
What fragrant rose in its sequestered bower
Has ever vied with her in spotlessness?
Truly the Lord, her God, the Holy One,
Has placed his tabernacle in the sun!

Thomas E. Burke, C.S.C.

Reading for Morning Prayer
Victory   1 Corinthians 15:52-57

The trumpet will sound, and the dead will be raised imperishable, and we will be changed. For this perishable body must put on imperishability, and this mortal body must put on immortality. . . . Then the saying that is written will be fulfilled: "Death has been swallowed up in victory. Where, O death, is your victory? Where, O death, is your sting?" The sting of death is sin, and the power of sin is the law. But thanks be to God, who gives us the victory through our Lord Jesus Christ.

Response

The holy Mother of God is exalted, alleluia!
—Above the choirs of angels, alleluia!

Antiphon for the Canticle of Zachary

Wise Virgin, where are you going, *
gleaming as bright as dawn?
Daughter of Zion, you are beauty itself,
serene as the moon,
and shining like the sun, alleluia!

Reading for Evening Prayer
Resurrection   John 11:20-27

When Martha heard that Jesus was coming, she went and met him, while Mary stayed at home. Martha said to Jesus, "Lord, if you had been here, my brother would not have died. But even now I know that God will give you whatever you ask of him." Jesus said to her, "Your brother will rise again." Martha said to him, "I know that

he will rise again in the resurrection on the last day."
Jesus said to her, "I am the resurrection and the life.
Those who believe in me, even though they die, will live,
and everyone who lives and believes in me will never die.
Do you believe this?" She said to him, "Yes, Lord, I
believe that you are the Messiah, the Son of God, the
one coming into the world."

Response

The Queen stands, O Lord, at your right hand, alleluia!
—Arrayed in vestments of gold, alleluia!

Antiphon for the Canticle of Mary

Mother of life, *
in giving birth, you preserved your virginity,
in falling asleep in death, you did not forsake us.
By your prayers, great Mother of God,
deliver our souls from death, alleluia!

Byzantine Troparion

Marian Litany

(see pages 299-312) followed by this Closing Prayer:

Father in heaven,
all creation rightly gives you praise
for all life and holiness come from you.
In the plan of your wisdom

she who bore Christ in her womb
was raised body and soul to glory
to be with you in heaven.
May we follow her example
in reflecting your holiness
and join with her hymn of endless praise.
We ask this through Christ our Lord.
—Amen.

Opening Prayer for August 15, *The Roman Missal.*

Blessing

May the great Mother of God, Mary most holy,
the queen of all saints,
+ intercede for us with the Lord.
—Amen.

September 8
The Nativity of Mary

Since the late fifth century, the Church of Jerusalem has venerated a place in the city where it was believed that Mary had been born. Both Rome and Byzantium and the Syrian Church celebrated this feast on September 8, the dedication date of the basilica of St. Mary's Birth. It was in this church, later called the basilica of St. Anne, that St. John of Damascus said in a homily: "Let everyone come to this feast; with joy let us celebrate the beginning of joy for the whole world! Today heaven begins on earth; today is the inauguration of salvation for the whole world."

Lessons for the Hour of Readings

(Insert in page 239)

1) Genesis 3:9-20

2) From a Homily of St. Augustine (354–430), Bishop of Hippo

   Dearly beloved: The much desired feast of Blessed Mary ever Virgin has come; so let our land, illumined by such a birth, be glad with great rejoicing. For she is the flower of the field from whom bloomed the precious Lily of the valley, through whose birth that nature inherited from our first parents is changed and guilt is blotted out. Eve mourned, Mary rejoiced. Eve carried tears in her heart; Mary, joy. For Eve gave birth to men of sin, Mary to the Innocent One. The mother of our race brought punishment upon the world, the Mother of our Lord brought salvation into the world. Eve was the author of sin, Mary the author of merit; Eve by killing was a hindrance, Mary by giving life was a help; Eve struck, and Mary healed. Disobedience is displaced by obedience, and fidelity atones for infidelity. Now let Mary play on musical instruments and let timbrels reverberate under the fleet fingers of this young Mother. Let joyous choirs sing together harmoniously, and let sweet songs be blended now with one melody and now with another. Hear how our timbrel-player has sung. For she said: "My soul magnifies the Lord and my spirit rejoices in God my Savior, because he has regarded the lowliness of his handmaid; for behold, henceforth all generations shall call me blessed; because he who is mighty has done great things for me." This miraculous new birth has utterly vanquished the root of aimless wanderings; Mary's canticle has ended the lamentations of Eve.

The Short Breviary (Collegeville, MN: The Liturgical Press, 1954).

Reading for Morning Prayer
Our Lady of Wisdom   Proverbs 8:22, 27-36

The Lord made me when he first began his work, at the birth of time, before his creation began. I was there when he built the heavens, when he fenced in the waters with a vault inviolable, when he fixed the sky overhead, and leveled the fountain-springs of the deep. Listen to me, then, you that are my children, that follow, to your happiness, in the paths I show you; listen to the teachings that will make you wise. Blessed are they who listen to me, keep vigil, day by day, at my threshold, watching till I open my doors. They who win me, win life, and drink deep of the Lord's favor.

(Knox translation)

Response

Today is the birthday of the Virgin-Mother, alleluia!
—Whose life illuminates the whole Church, alleluia!

Antiphon for the Canticle of Zachary

Great Mother of God, *
your birth brings joy to the whole universe,
for from you arose the Sun of righteousness, Christ our Lord,

who broke the curse and conferred the blessing,
who abolished death and brought us life eternal, alleluia!

Byzantine antiphon

Reading for Evening Prayer
Mary's Ancestry   Matthew 1:1-2, 5-6, 16

An account of the genealogy of Jesus the Messiah, the son of David, the son of Abraham. Abraham was the father of Isaac, and Isaac the father of Jacob, and Jacob the father of Judah and his brothers . . . and Obed the father of Jesse, and Jesse the father of King David. And David was the father of Solomon by the wife of Uriah. . . . And Jacob the father of Joseph the husband of Mary, of whom Jesus was born, who is called the Messiah.

Response

Blessed are you, O Virgin Mary, alleluia!
—For you put your faith in Christ your Son, alleluia!

Antiphon for the Canticle of Mary

Mary's canticle of joy
* has put an end to the lamentations of Eve, alleluia!

Marian Litany

(see pages 299-312) followed by this Closing Prayer:

The world's redemption dawns, O God,
with the birth of our Savior's mother.
May an increase of peace be the reward
of those who celebrate her birthday each year.
We ask this through Christ our Lord.
—Amen.

Blessing

May the Virgin Mary mild
+ bless us with her holy Child.
—Amen.

December 8
Mary's Immaculate Conception

The feast of St. Anne's conception of her predestined daughter originated in the East and first appeared in the West in the seventh century. After a short time it faded from view and only reappeared in England in the twelfth century. Despite the opposition of great saints and theologians like Bernard of Clairvaux and Thomas Aquinas, it gradually spread to many dioceses and religious orders and was fixed on December 8 by the Council of Basel in 1438. In 1854, after consultation with the universal church, Pope Pius IX declared it a dogma: "By the singular favor and privilege of Almighty God, in view of the merits of Jesus Christ, the Savior of the human race, the Blessed Virgin Mary was preserved free from the stain of original sin from the first instance of her conception" [in the womb of her mother].

Lessons for the Hour of Readings

(insert in page 239)

1) Romans 5:12-21

2) The Immaculate One

   From the first moment of Mary's human existence until her assumption into heaven, every detail of her life that revelation has provided is "a type of what is to come." The church is symbolized in Mary. [This is] the first and underlying mystery of her life, namely that Mary in the first instant of her conception, in virtue of the redemptive death to come of her divine son, was preserved free from all stain of original sin. She possessed from the beginning also, precisely as a member of the human race redeemed by Christ, the gift of sanctifying grace which was destined originally for the whole human race from Adam and Eve, and restored to every believer by the death of Christ, the son of Mary. Thus it is that Mary Immaculate is already an essential symbol of the restoration to grace, a work which began on the cross and which will have its entire fulfillment at the end of time by presenting to the eternal Father Adam's family, redeemed into the one glorified Body of Christ: a symbol therefore of the church. This is how the early Fathers saw in Mary Immaculate the *Ecclesia Immaculata*, and in this figure of the Church Immaculate the glorious conclusion of the work of redemption, which will be revealed on that day when God "who is able to preserve you without sin" will "present you spotless *(immaculatos)* before the presence of his glory with exceeding joy in the coming of our Lord Jesus Christ" (Jude 24).

Hugo Rahner, S.J., *Our Lady and the Church* (New York: Random House, 1961).

Reading for Morning Prayer
Mary Is All Fair   Isaiah 61:10-11

I will greatly rejoice in the LORD, my whole being shall exult in my God; for he has clothed me with the garments of salvation, he has covered me with the robe of righteousness, as a bridegroom decks himself with a garland, and as a bride adorns herself with her jewels. For as the earth brings forth its shoots, and as a garden causes what is sown in it to spring up, so the Lord GOD will cause righteousness and praise to spring up before all the nations.

Response

Death came through Eve, alleluia!
—Life through Mary, alleluia!

Antiphon for the Canticle of Zachary

The Lord God said to the serpent: *
I will put enmity between you and the woman,
and between your offspring and hers, alleluia!

Reading for Evening Prayer
The Bride of Christ   Song of Songs 2:10-14

Arise, my love, my fair one, and come away; for now the winter is past, the rain is over and gone. The flowers appear on the earth; the time of singing has come, and the voice of the turtledove is heard in our land. The fig tree puts forth its figs, and the vines are in blossom; they give forth fragrance. Arise, my love, my fair one, and come away. O my dove, in the clefts of the rock, in the covert of the cliff, let me see your face, let me hear your voice; for your voice is sweet, and your face is lovely.

Response

You are all fair, O Mary, alleluia!
—And no stain of sin mars your loveliness, alleluia!

Antiphon for the Canticle of Mary

You shall be a crown of beauty, O Virgin Mary, *
a royal diadem in the hand of your God, alleluia!

Marian Litany

(see pages 299-312) followed by this Closing Prayer:

Father of all holiness,
by the foreseen merits of Jesus her Savior,
you preserved Mary his Mother from all sin
even at the first moment of her conception.

By her unceasing intercession
may the Church be holy and without blemish
and stand rejoicing in your sight
when Christ comes again in glory
to judge the living and the dead.
We ask this through the same Christ our Lord.
—Amen.

Blessing

By the merits and prayers of Mary Immaculate
and of all the saints in glory,
may the Lord + bring us into his heavenly mansions.
—Amen.

December 12
Our Lady of Guadalupe

Shortly after the brutal conquest of Mexico, the Blessed Virgin appeared in the form of an Indian maiden, in December 1531, to a recent Aztec convert, Juan Diego. After she convinced Bishop Zumarraga of Mexico City by a gift of roses and the impression of her image on the Juan Diego's *tilma*, he established a shrine in her honor on the hill of Tepeyac. The picture itself delighted the conquered Aztecs and awed the conquering Spaniards. Because of the flood of new converts that ensued, Our Lady of Guadalupe, as she came to be called, is considered the Apostle of the Aztecs. As her shrine and pilgrimage grew, the papacy declared her the Patroness of Mexico and the Empress of the Americas. For many she is the primary defender of the all too numerous poor and oppressed of Latin America; her "fundamental option" is clear!

Lessons for the Hour of Readings

(insert in page 239)

1) Matthew 25:31-46; or Revelation 21:1-27

2) Mary's Radical Openness to the Spirit

   "I am the handmaid of the Lord. Let it be done to me according to your word" (Luke 1:38). Contemplation of the Blessed Virgin Mary leads us to reflection on what our faith should look like. In celebrating the mystery of the Incarnation, we are witnesses to the first act of faith and hope, we see a God of love who chooses one for us. On a very practical level, the *fiat* of Mary, the joyful "yes!," must serve as a model to believers.

Mary's greatness lies in her radical openness to the Holy Spirit. Her faith is boundless. St. Augustine states: "Mary's happiness is much greater for having conceived Jesus Christ in faith than in having given birth to the Savior in the flesh. The maternal bonds that united Mary to her divine Son would have been pointless had she not borne more happily in her heart." (*De virginitate* in M.D. Philippe, O.P., *Mystery of Mary, Model of Christian Life,* Community of St. John, 1958.)

She is blessed because she believed. Through her *fiat,* Mary's spirit in a dynamic and intimate sense, submits to the will of God. In this divine surrender to the will of God, there is no reservation, restriction or limitation to this gift of her spirit and heart.... Filled with joy at the impending birth, Mary shares her gladness with Elizabeth and pours out both her joys and hopes in her *Magnificat.* ... In this canticle, Mary urges us not to be afraid of giving ourselves enthusiastically, joyfully to God. The words of the *Magnificat* are full of longing and love for God. Spiritual inebriation reawakens our desire for pure praise, awestruck wonder of God's majesty and holiness.

In the second part of the *Magnificat*, Mary looks out upon the world into which her Son will be born. Now we see a joining of a spiritual rapture to a critical perspective on the world. Mary describes a radical reversal of human positions: On the one hand, the rich and the powerful; on the other, the humble and the hungry. . . . Mary speaks to the poor and humble because she is poor and humble. In her song of praise, we see God raising all those who suffer nearer to his Heart just as Mary held the Christ Child to her heart.

The Houston Catholic Worker (Dec. 1998) alt.

Reading for Morning Prayer
Hunger and Thirst   Sirach 24:19-22

Come to me, you who desire me, and eat your fill of my fruits. For the memory of me is sweeter than honey, and the possession of me sweeter than the honeycomb. Those who eat of me will hunger for more, and those who drink of me will thirst for more. Whoever obeys me will not be put to shame, and those who work with me will not sin.

Response

The Almighty fills the hungry with good things, alleluia!

—And sends the rich away empty, alleluia!

Antiphon for the Canticle of Zachary

Blessed be the great Mother of God, * Mary most holy, who scatters the proud in their conceit, alleluia!

Reading for Evening Prayer
Mary of Nazareth   Luke 1:26-28

The angel Gabriel was sent by God to a town in Galilee called Nazareth, to a virgin engaged to a man whose name was Joseph, of the house of David. The virgin's name was Mary. And the angel came to her and said, "Greetings, favored one! The Lord is with you."

Response

My spirit rejoices in God my Savior, alleluia!
—For all generations will call me blessed, alleluia!

Antiphon for the Canticle of Mary

Radiant Mother of God, * comforter of the afflicted and cause of our joy, come to our assistance, alleluia!

Marian Litany

(see pages 299-312) followed by this Closing Prayer:

God of power and mercy,
you blessed the Americas at Tepeyac
with the presence of the Virgin Mary of Guadalupe.
May her prayers help all men and women
to accept each other as brothers and sisters.
Through your justice present in our hearts
may social justice and peace reign in the world.
Please grant this through Christ our Lord.
—Amen.

Book of Mary (Washington, D.C.: United States Catholic Conference, 1987).

Blessing

May the Virgin Mary of Guadalupe
+ be the joy and consolation of her people.
—Amen.

An Hour of

Marian Readings

for the

Christian Year

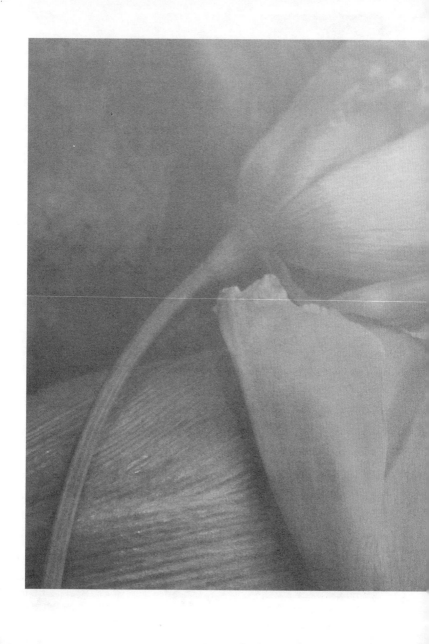

$\mathcal{A}$ COMMON OFFICE THROUGHOUT THE YEAR

The Night Office was originally created as a nocturnal devotion of psalms, readings, meditation, and contemplation. Now called the Hour of Readings, it may be used at any time of the day or night but will be particularly useful during the long hours of the night for those who are retired, incapacitated, ill, or who find they sleep badly for one reason or another. Such wakefulness may prove to be a God-given opportunity for prayer, spiritual reading, meditation, and intercession. When the Hour of Readings is not used, the readings themselves may be used at Morning and Evening Prayer in place of the ordinary ones.

This hour will probably be used mostly by individuals, but for group use follow the directions given in the introduction and during Morning and Evening Prayer for Advent, pages 37-56.

O Lord, + open my lips,
—And my mouth shall proclaim your praise.
O Mary, you are more worthy of honor than the cherubim
—And far more glorious than the seraphim.
You gave birth to the Word of God for our sake.
—O great Mother of God, we acclaim you!

Psalm 95:1-7 A Call to Prayer

Antiphon   Hail, Mary, * full of grace, the Lord is with you.

1. Come, ring out our joy to the LORD;
    hail the rock who saves us.
    Let us come before God, giving thanks,
    with songs let us hail the Lord.

Antiphon   Hail, Mary, full of grace, the Lord is with you.

2. A mighty God is the LORD,
    a great king above all gods,
    in whose hands are the depths of the earth;
    the heights of the mountains as well.

The sea belongs to God, who made it
and the dry land shaped by his hands.

Antiphon   Hail, Mary, full of grace, the Lord is with
you.

3.   Come in; let us bow and bend low;
let us kneel before the God who made us
for this is our God and we
the people who belong to his pasture,
the flock that is led by his hand.

Antiphon   Hail, Mary, full of grace, the Lord is with
you.

4.   Glory to the holy and undivided Trinity:
now and always and for ever and ever. Amen.

Antiphon   Hail, Mary, full of grace, the Lord is with
you.

Marian Hymn

1.   O glorious Lady, throned in rest,
Amidst the starry host above,
Who gave sweet nurture from your breast
To God, with pure maternal love.

2.   O gate, through which has passed the King,
O hall, whence Light shone through the gloom:
The ransomed nations praise and sing
Life given from the Virgin's womb.

3. O Lord, the Virgin born, to you
    Eternal praise and laud are due
    Whom with the Father we adore
    And Spirit blest for evermore. Amen.

Text: *O gloriosa femina*, attributed to Venantius Fortunatus (530–609), trans. John Mason Neale (1818–1866), alt.

Psalms for the Five Seasons

Advent
Psalm 19 The Light of the World

Antiphon   The Dawn from on high * shall break upon
            us.

1. The heavens proclaim the glory of God,
    and the firmament shows forth the work of God's
        hands.
    Day unto day takes up the story
    and night unto night makes known the message.

2. No speech, no word, no voice is heard
    yet their span extends through all the earth,
    their words to the utmost bounds of the world.

3. There God has placed a tent for the sun;

    it comes forth like a bridegroom coming from
        his tent,
    rejoices like a champion to run its course.

4. At the ending of the sky is the rising of the sun;
    to the furthest end of the sky is its course.
    There is nothing concealed from its burning heat.

Antiphon   The Dawn from on high shall break upon
            us.

Psalm Prayer

Let us pray (*pause for silent prayer*).
Lord Jesus Christ, Sun of Righteousness,
shine on those who sit in darkness
and in the shadow of death,
for you are the morning star of the universe,
the light and life of the world,
and we glorify you and your Virgin Mother,
now and for ever.
—Amen.

Christmas
Psalm 72 The Messianic King

Antiphon   Blest is the womb that bore you, O Christ, *
            and the breasts that nursed you, alleluia!

1. O God, give your judgment to the king,
    to a king's son your justice,
    that he may judge your people in justice
    and your poor in right judgment.

2. May the mountains bring forth peace for the people
   and the hills, justice.
   May he defend the poor of the people
   and save the children of the needy.

3. He shall endure like the sun and the moon
   from age to age.
   He shall descend like rain on the meadows,
   like raindrops on the earth.

4. In his days justice shall flourish
   and peace till the moon fails.
   He shall rule from sea to sea,
   from the Great River to earth's bounds.

5. Before him his enemies shall fall,
   his foes lick the dust.
   The kings of Tarshish and the seacoasts
   shall pay him tribute.

6. The kings of Sheba and Seba
   shall bring him gifts.
   Before him all rulers shall fall prostrate,
   all nations shall serve him.

7. For he shall save the people when they cry
   and the needy who are helpless.
   He will have pity on the weak
   and save the lives of the poor.

8. From oppression he will rescue their lives,
   to him their blood is dear.

They shall pray for him without ceasing
and bless him all the day.

9. May corn be abundant in the land
   to the peaks of the mountains.
   May its fruit rustle like Lebanon;
   may people flourish in the cities
   like grass on the earth.

10. May his name be blessed for ever
    and endure like the sun.
    Every tribe shall be blessed in him,
    all nations bless his name.

Antiphon   Blest is the womb that bore you, O Christ,
           and the breasts that nursed you, alleluia!

Psalm Prayer

Let us pray *(pause for silent prayer).*
Anointed Son of God,
rule from sea to sea
and to the very ends of the earth.
Defend the poor, set their children free,
save their lives from violence,
lives that are precious in your sight.
Let your glory fill the world,
now and for ever.
—Amen.

Assumptiontide
Psalm 45 A Wedding Song

Psalm 45 is an example of a wedding song of a King of Israel turned into a love song between God and Israel, Christ and the Church, and here between King Jesus and Queen Mary.

Antiphon   Adorn your bridal chamber, O Mary, *
          and welcome Christ the King.

1. My heart overflows with noble words.
   To the king I must speak the song I have made,
   my tongue as nimble as the pen of a scribe.

The King

2. You are the fairest of the men on earth
   and graciousness is poured upon your lips,
   because God has blessed you for evermore.

3. O mighty one, gird your sword upon your thigh;
   in splendor and state ride on in triumph
   for the cause of truth and goodness and right.

4. Take aim with your bows in your dread right hand.
   Your arrows are sharp, peoples fall beneath you.
   The foes of the king fall down and lose heart.

5. Your throne, O God, shall endure for ever.
   A scepter of justice is the scepter of your kingdom.
   Your love is for justice, your hatred for evil.

6. Therefore God, your God, has anointed you
   with the oil of gladness above other kings;
   your robes are fragrant with aloes and myrrh.

7. From the ivory palace you are greeted with music.
   The daughters of kings are among your loved ones.
   On your right hand stands the queen in gold of
   Ophir.

The Queen

8. Listen, O daughter, give ear to my words:
   forget your own people and your father's house.
   So will the king desire your beauty;
   he is your lord, pay homage to him.

9. And the people of Tyre shall come with gifts,
   the richest of the people shall seek your favor.
   The daughter of the king is clothed with splendor,
   her robes embroidered with pearls set in gold.

10. She is led to the king with her maiden companions.
    They are escorted amid gladness and joy;
    they pass within the palace of the king.

11. Children shall be yours in place of your forebears;
    you will make them rulers over all the earth.
    May this song make your name ever remembered.
    May the peoples praise you from age to age.

Antiphon   Adorn your bridal chamber, O Mary,
            and welcome Christ the King.

Psalm Prayer

Let us pray *(pause for silent prayer).*
Great Mother of God,
through the Father's pleasure
and the Spirit's power,
you received in your womb the Word,
the wisdom and the power of God.
Enkindle our love for your Son,
and make our lives pleasing to him,
so that we may come to share
in your happiness on high
and see you in the radiance of your Son,
to whom be honor, glory, and power,
with the Father and the Holy Spirit,
now and for ever.
—Amen.

Lent and the Paschal Triduum
Psalm 22 The Passion, Death, and Resurrection

Antiphon   From my mother's womb * you have been
            my God.

1. My God, my God, why have you forsaken me?
   You are far from my plea and the cry of my distress.
   O my God, I call by day and you give no reply;
   I call by night and I find no peace.

2. Yet you, O God, are holy,
   enthroned on the praises of Israel.
   In you our forebears put their trust;
   they trusted and you set them free.
   When they cried to you, they escaped.
   In you they trusted and never in vain.

3. But I am a worm and no man,
   the butt of all, laughing-stock of the people.
   All who see me deride me.
   They curl their lips, they toss their heads.
   "He trusted in the LORD, let him save him,
   and release him if this is his friend."

4. Yes, it was you who took me from the womb,
   entrusted me to my mother's breast.
   To you I was committed from my birth,
   from my mother's womb you have been my God.
   Do not leave me alone in my distress;
   Come close, there is none else to help.

5. Many bulls have surrounded me,
   fierce bulls of Bashan close me in.
   Against me they open wide their jaws,
   like lions, rending and roaring.

6. Like water I am poured out,
   disjointed are all my bones.
   My heart has become like wax,
   it is melted within my breast.

Parched as burnt clay is my throat,
my tongue cleaves to my jaws.

7. Many dogs have surrounded me,
a band of the wicked beset me.
They tear holes in my hands and my feet
and lay me in the dust of death.

8. I can count every one of my bones.
These people stare at me and gloat;
they divide my clothing among them.
They cast lots for my robe.

9. O LORD, do not leave me alone,
my strength, make haste to help me!
Rescue my soul from the sword,
my life from the grip of these dogs.
Save my life from the jaws of these lions,
my soul from the horns of these oxen.

10. I will tell your name to my people
and praise you where they are assembled.
"You who fear the LORD give praise;
all children of Jacob, give glory.
Revere God, children of Israel.

11. For God has never despised
nor scorned the poverty of the poor,
nor looked away from them,
but has heard the poor when they cried."

12. You are my praise in the great assembly.
    My vows I will pay before those who fear God.
    The poor shall eat and shall have their fill.
    Those who seek the LORD shall praise the LORD.
    May their hearts live for ever and ever.

13. All the earth shall remember and return to the
        Lord,
    all families of the nations shall bow down in awe;
    for the kingdom is the Lord's, who is ruler of all.
    They shall bow down in awe, all the mighty of the
        earth,
    all who must die and go down to the dust.

14. My soul shall live for God and my children too
        shall serve.
    They shall tell of the Lord to generations yet to
        come;
    declare to those unborn, the faithfulness of God.
    "These things the Lord has done."

Antiphon   From my mother's womb you have been my
            God.

Psalm Prayer

Let us pray *(pause for silent prayer)*.
Lord Jesus, man of sorrows,
and acquainted with grief,
we stand in awe before your bitter Passion

and with your sorrowful Mother,
shed tears of compassion
in the face of the five precious wounds
in your hands, feet, and side.
By your pierced and broken heart
and by the tears of your dear Mother,
may we glory in your saving Cross
and in the rescuing God
who delivered you out of death
and had you proclaim to all sinners:
"God saves!"
Blessed be God for ever!
—Amen.

Easter
Psalm 76 God Is a Warrior, Rome Quails

Antiphon   For fear of the angel * the guards shook
          and became like dead men, alleluia!

1.   God, you are known in Judah;
    in Israel your name is great.
    You set up your tent in Jerusalem
    and your dwelling place in Zion.
    It was there you broke the flashing arrows,
    the shield, the sword, the armor.

2. You, O Lord, are resplendent,
   more majestic than the everlasting mountains.
   The warriors, despoiled, slept in death;
   the hands of the soldiers were powerless.
   At your threat, O God of Jacob,
   horse and rider lay stunned.

3. You, you alone, strike terror.
   Who shall stand when your anger is roused?
   You uttered your sentence from the heavens;
   the earth in terror was still
   when you arose to judge,
   to save the humble of the earth.

4. Human anger will serve to praise you;
   those who survive it rejoice in you.
   Make vows to your God and fulfill them.
   Let all pay tribute to the one who strikes terror,
   who cuts short the breath of rulers,
   who strikes terror in the leaders of the earth.

Antiphon   For fear of the angel the guards shook
            and became like dead men, alleluia!

Psalm Prayer

Let us pray *(pause for silent prayer)*.
Lord Jesus Christ,
when God raised you from the grave,
the fearful guards were terrified

and became like dead men.
Make us, who believe in your resurrection,
confident of our victory over death and the grave
because of the stunning power of your Father.
You live and reign, O risen Christ, now and for ever.
—Amen.

A Marian Anthem for the Nine Feasts
Judith 13:18-20; 15:9 (TEV)

Antiphon   All generations * will call me blessed!

1.   The Most High God has blessed you
      more than any other woman on earth.
      How worthy of praise is the Lord God
      who created heaven and earth!
      He guided you as you cut off the head
      of our deadliest enemy.

Antiphon   All generations will call me blessed!

2.   Your trust in God will never be forgotten
      by those who tell of God's power.
      May God give you everlasting honor
      for what you have done.

Antiphon   All generations will call me blessed!

3.   May God reward you with blessings,
      because you remained faithful to him

238

and did not hesitate to risk your own life
to relieve the oppression of your people.

Antiphon   All generations will call me blessed!

4.   You are Jerusalem's crowning glory,
       the heroine of Israel,
       the pride and joy of our people!

Antiphon   All generations will call me blessed!

Psalm Prayer

Let us pray *(pause for silent prayer)*.
Holy Mary, mother of the Messiah,
like the heroine Judith of old,
you risked everything for God's people
and became renowned for ever.
May we never forget your trust in God
as we rely on your prayers for us.
Your Son is God's Son,
who lives and reigns for ever and ever.
—Amen.

Reading

Insert appropriate readings from one of the five liturgical seasons or from the nine feasts. A period of meditation follows each reading.

A Hymn of Praise to Our Lady
(*Te Matrem Laudamus*)

A. We praise you as our Mother, *
    we acclaim you as our blessed Lady.
    All the earth reveres you,
    the daughter of the Eternal Father.

    The hosts of heaven and all the angelic powers
    sing your praise:
    the angels join in the dance,
    the archangels applaud, the virtues give praise,
    the principalities rejoice, the powers exult,
    the dominations delight, the thrones make festival,
    the cherubim and seraphim cry out unceasingly:

    Holy, holy, holy is the great Mother of God,
    Mary most holy;
    the blessed fruit of your womb
    is the glory of heaven and earth.

    The glorious choir of apostles,
    the noble company of prophets,
    the white-robed army of martyrs,
    all sing your praise.

    The holy Church throughout the world
    celebrates you:
    the daughter of infinite Majesty,

the mother of God's true and only Son,
the bride of the Spirit of truth and consolation.

B. You bore Christ, the King of glory,
the eternal Son of the Father.
When he took our nature to set us free,
he did not spurn your virgin womb.
When he overcame death's sting,
he assumed you into heaven.

You now sit with your Son
at God's right hand in glory.
Intercede for us, O Virgin Mary,
when he comes to be our judge.

Help your chosen people
bought with his precious blood.
And bring us with all the saints
into glory everlasting.

C. Save your people, O holy Virgin,
and bless your inheritance.
Rule them and uphold them,
now and for ever.

Day by day we salute you;
we acclaim you unceasingly.
In your goodness pray for us sinners;
have mercy on us poor sinners.

> May your mercy sustain us always,
> for we put our trust in you.
> In you, dear Mother, do we trust;
> defend us now and for ever.

Translated and adapted from several medieval manuscripts of the twelfth and thirteenth centuries.

Closing Prayers for the Five Seasons

Advent:

Creator and redeemer of the human race,
your Word became flesh
in the womb of the Virgin Mary
for us and for our salvation.
May we who, by baptism, share the divinity of Christ,
participate in the merits and prayers
of the Mother of God and of all the saints in glory;
through the same Christ Jesus our Lord.
—Amen.

Christmas:

God our Father,
may we always have the prayers
of the Virgin Mother Mary,
for through Jesus Christ her Son

you bring us light and salvation;
he lives and reigns with you and the Holy Spirit,
one God, for ever and ever.
—Amen.

Opening Prayer for January 1, *The Roman Missal.*

Assumptiontide:

Immaculate Lady, remember your Christian servants;
present the prayers and the hopes of us all to the Lord.
Confirm our faith, unite the churches,
give peace to the world, save us from all dangers and
    trials,
and beg for each of us that the day of judgment
may not be a day of condemnation.
For you are one who has done great things among us
and who never ceased to do them;
holy is your name,
which is blessed by angels and human beings
from generation to generation,
now and to the ages of ages.
—Amen.

St. Germanus of Constantinople (died ca. 742), *Encomium on the Dormition of Mary,* Homily 2, 11, trans. Brian Daley, *On the Dormition of Mary,* pp. 178-179.

Lent:

Lord Jesus Christ,
at whose blessed passion,
as old Simeon had foretold,
a sword of sorrow pierced your Mother's soul
as she stood beneath the cross:
grant that we who reverently recall her sorrows
may reap the happy fruit of your saving sufferings.
You are our blessed Savior, now and forever.
—Amen.

Easter:

Great and rescuing God,
by the resurrection of your Son, our Lord Jesus Christ,
you gave joy to the world.
Grant that by the prayers of his Mother, the Blessed
    Virgin Mary,
we may obtain the happiness of everlasting life;
through the same Christ our Lord.
—Amen.

Ascription of Praise

Praise, hymns, and glory belong to God:
Father, Son, and Holy Spirit,
through all the ages of ages.
—Amen.

Readings for the Five Seasons of the Christian Year

Readings for the Season of Advent (See the Table of Feasts, page 30)

Bible Readings for the Season of Advent:

The Sign of Emmanuel	Isaiah 7:10-16
The Messianic King	Isaiah 9:1b-7
The Messiah	Isaiah 11:1-10
The Messianic Age	Isaiah 11:10-16
God's Glory	Isaiah 35:1-10
God's Coming	Isaiah 40:1-11
The Servant of God	Isaiah 42:1-9
The Servant of God	Isaiah 49:1-7; 49:8-13; 49:14-21
Jesus' royal descent and the annunciation to St. Joseph	Matthew 1:1-25
The annunciation and birth of John the Baptist	Luke 1:5-25, 57-80
The annunciation of the angel Gabriel to the Virgin Mary	Luke 1:26-56

Pause for meditation after the first reading.

Second Readings from the Fathers
and other spiritual writers:

1. Mary and Eve

    Just as it was through a virgin who disobeyed that
    humanity was stricken and fell and died, so too it was
    through the Virgin, who obeyed the word of God,
    that we, resuscitated by life, received life. For the
    Lord came to seek back the lost sheep, and it was we
    who were lost; and therefore he did not become some
    other formation, but he likewise, of her that was
    descended of Adam, preserved the likeness of
    formation; for Adam had necessarily to be restored in
    Christ, that mortality be absorbed in immortality,
    and Eve in Mary, that a virgin, become the advocate
    of a virgin, should undo and destroy virginal
    disobedience by virginal obedience.

St. Irenaeus of Lyons (ca. 130–ca. 200), *Proof of the Apostolic Preaching 33,*
Ancient Christian Writers 16 (Westminster, MD: The Newman Press,
1952), p. 69 alt.

2. The Annunciation

    In fear of God let us stand to praise
    the grace and glory of our Lady,
    the channel of joy, of more beauty
    than the thousand eyes of the Cherubim
    or the multiple wings of the Seraphim.
    The Father looked down from heaven

east and west, north and south,
into every end of the earth.
Smelling the savor of every scent
he found nothing like you where he went;
And of your prepared singularity
he made his beloved the Baby.
You are the loom from which Emmanuel took
his robe of flesh; the warp and the woof
are yours and Adam's; the Word himself,
Jesus Christ is the shuttle; the long thread
in the warp is the high Godhead.
The Spirit wove this wonderful web,
seven curtains of fiery red,
round the throne and Cherubim,
pitched this in the narrow room
of a young bride, not burning
your virgin womb, nor turning
your milk in the same flame.

George Every after the Ethiopian Anaphora of Mary in J.M. Rodwell, *Ethiopian Liturgies and Hymns* (1864) in *The Time of the Spirit* (Crestwood, NY: St. Vladimir's Seminary Press, 1984), p. 138.

3. The Flower From the Rod of Jesse
   "There shall come forth a rod out of the root of Jesse, and a flower shall rise up out of his root, and the spirit of the Lord shall rest upon him" (Isaiah 11:1-2). We believe that the holy Virgin Mary is the new shoot that sprouts from the root of Jesse . . . as

we read of him earlier in Isaiah 7:14: "Look, the virgin is with child and shall bear a son, and shall call him Emmanuel," and the branch that flowers is the Lord our Savior, who says in the *Canticle of Canticles* 2:1: "I am the flower of the field and the lily of the valley." It is on this flowering branch that the Spirit of the Lord shall rest, the branch that springs from the root of Jesse through the Virgin Mary; in him "all the fullness of the Godhead lives in bodily form" (Colossians 2:9) and not in part, as in the case of others who had been sanctified by the Spirit. As the Nazarenes state it in their gospel written in Hebrew: "The whole fountain of the Holy Spirit shall fall on him; the Lord is a spirit and where the Spirit of the Lord lives, freedom lives."

St. Jerome (ca. 342–420), from the *Tridentine Breviary*, 2nd Sunday of Advent, Matins, 2nd Nocturn, trans. WGS.

4. On the Incarnation
    When the holy Virgin offered her womb, the Word rushed in through her sense of hearing; the Holy Spirit built a living temple; the Most High emptied himself, taking the form of a slave, and, finally, the Virgin's womb carried the mystery of the divine economy. O womb wider than the heavens! O birth pregnant with salvation! O womb, who were the bridal chamber of the clay and the potter! O mystery, which I do not know how to explain!

O birth, who gave and announced to the people, not the beginning of divine existence, not a change of nature, not a lessening of power, not a separation from the eternal Parent, but the substantial union of God and the flesh, the blessing of birth and the coming of God, the wonder hidden in God from all ages, the unfathomable mystery of the two natures, the end of the curse, the destruction of the condemnation, the eternal existence of a single and unique Son and his generation from the Virgin according to the flesh, the adoration of all creation.

St. Proclus, Patriarch of Constantinople (434–446), *Homily 4 on the Nativity of the Lord*, trans. Thomas Buffer in Luigi Gambero, SM, *Mary and the Fathers of the Church* (San Francisco: Ignatius Press, 1999), p. 258.

5. The Two Births
    Son of God, who is the ineffable Word,
    give me a word which sings your praise abundantly.
    The Father begot you beyond time, without a
        beginning,
    and again the Virgin Mother bore you without
        explanation.
    The Father in his love and by the grace that is in his
        nature,
    sent his Son to us that in the end He might be Son
        also to us.
    While he was born beyond time according to his
        essence,

at the end of time he became a babe for us.

He has a Father, and by his grace he has taken a
    mother for himself;

when he was born he descended and he dwelt in her,

that he might be her Offspring.

He chose for himself a Virgin, who was betrothed
    and preserved;

she was holy, modest, and vigilant.

He descended and dwelt in the blessed one, most fair;

her womb was sealed, her body was holy, and her soul
    was limpid.

Jacob of Serug (ca. 451–521), *Homily Concerning the Annunciation of the Mother of God,* trans. Mary Hansbury, *On the Mother of God* (Crestwood, NY: St. Vladimir's Seminary Press, 1998).

Readings for the Season of Christmas (December 25-February 2)

Bible Readings for the Season of Christmas:

Isaiah 41:17-20	Is. 42:1-20
Is. 43:1-13	Is. 43:18-28
Is. 44:1-8, 22-23	Is. 45:1-13
Is. 46:3-13	Is. 48:1-11
Is. 49:1-7	Is. 49:10-18
Is. 49:22-26	Is. 51:1-11
Is. 52:7-15	Is. 55:1-5
Is. 55:10-13	Is. 60:1-6
Is. 61:1-4, 10-11	Is. 66:10-16
Micah 4:1-9	Micah 5:1-9
Micah 7:14-20	
The Birth and Childhood of Jesus	Luke 2:1-52
The Magi and the Flight Into Egypt	Matthew 2:1-23
A Wedding in Cana of Galilee	John 2:1-11
John the Baptist	Luke 3:1-22

Pause for meditation after the first reading.

Second Readings from the Fathers and other spiritual writers:

1. Mary and Eve

    Christ is born of the Virgin, in order that the disobedience caused by the serpent might be destroyed in the same manner in which it had originated. For Eve, an undefiled virgin, conceived the word of the serpent and brought forth disobedience and death. But the Virgin Mary, filled with faith and joy, when the angel Gabriel announced to her that the Spirit of the Lord would come upon her, and the power of the Most High would overshadow her, and therefore the Holy One born of her would be the Son of God, answered: "Be it done unto me according to your word" (Luke 1:38). And, indeed, she gave birth to him, concerning whom we have shown so many passages of Scripture were written, and by whom God destroys both the serpent and those angels and humans who have become like the serpent, but frees from death those who repent of their sins and believe in Christ.

St. Justin Martyr (ca. 100–ca. 165), Dialogue with Trypho, chap. 100 in *The Writings of Justin Martyr*, ed. T. Falls (New York: Christian Heritage, 1948), pp. 304-305.

2. Christ's Two Birthdays

    He who had brought all things into existence, was brought into existence in the midst of all things. He made the day—he came into the light of day. He who was before time, set his seal upon time. Christ the Lord was forever without beginning with the Father; but look what he is today! It is his birthday. Whose birthday? The Lord's. He has a birthday? Yes, he has. "In the beginning was the Word and the Word was with God" (John 1:1)—He has a birthday? Yes, he has. If he had not been begotten as a human being, we would not attain our divine rebirth; for he was born that we might be reborn.

Christ has been born; let no one hesitate to be reborn. Christ has been begotten, but without need of being begotten anew. Indeed, for whom was a second begetting necessary, if not for him whose first begetting was condemned? May his mercy, therefore, be given to our hearts.

His mother carried him in her womb; let us carry him in our hearts. By the Incarnation of Christ was a virgin made fruitful; let our breasts be made fruitful by the faith of Christ. She gave birth to the Savior; let us give birth to good deeds. Let us not be sterile, let our souls be fruitful for God.

St. Augustine of Hippo (354–430), trans. T.C. Lawler, *Sermons for Christmas and Epiphany, Ancient Christian Writers 15* (New York: Newman Press, 1952), pp. 98-99.

3. Christ's Birthday

Let us celebrate the Lord's birthday with the enthusiasm that we should give it. Let men rejoice; let women rejoice. Christ was born Man; he was born of a Woman. Both sexes have been honored. Let him, therefore, who had been condemned before in the first man, now become a follower of the Second Man. A woman had been the cause of our death; a woman, again, gave birth to life for us. "The likeness of sinful flesh" (Romans 8:3) was born to purify the sinful flesh. For that reason do not let the flesh be found with sin, but let sin die that nature may live; for he was born without sin, that he who was with sin might be reborn. . . .

Rejoice, you who are just. It is the birthday of him who justifies.

Rejoice, you who are weak and sick. It is the birthday of him who makes us well.

Rejoice, you who are in captivity. It is the birthday of the Redeemer.

Rejoice, you who are slaves. It is the birthday of the Master.

Rejoice, you who are free. It is the birthday of him who makes us free.

Rejoice, you Christians all. It is Christ's birthday.

By his birth of an earth-born mother he hallowed this one day who by his birth of the Father was the Creator of all ages. . . . Rightly did the prophets announce that he was to be born, and the heavens and the angels that he had been born. He whose hands governed the world, lay in the manger; and speechless Infant that he was, he was also the Word. Him whom the heavens cannot contain, the womb of one woman bore. She ruled our Ruler; she carried him in whom we are; she gave milk to our Bread.

From a Christmas Homily of St. Augustine of Hippo (354–430), trans. T.C. Lawler, *Ancient Christian Writers 15*, pp. 73-75.

4. Glory to God in the Highest

When the gospel was read, we heard the words with which the angels announced to the shepherds that the Lord Jesus Christ was born of the Virgin: "Glory to God in the highest heaven, and on earth peace to those whom God has chosen." Festive words these are, words of felicitation addressed not alone to the Woman whose womb gave birth to the Child, but to the human race for whom the Virgin gave birth to the Savior. To be sure, it was but right and entirely becoming, that this new Mother, who had begotten the Lord of heaven and earth and who had remained a virgin after the Child was born, should have her childbearing proclaimed not by mere women with human solemnities, but by angels singing the praises of God. And now let us too say, and let us say it with all the rejoicing of which we are capable: "Glory to God in the highest heaven, and on earth peace to those whom God has chosen." And let us with our best effort study and examine these divine words, these praises of God, the joy of the angels, and meditate on them with faith and hope and charity. For as we believe and hope and desire, so shall we also be "glory to God in the highest," when in the resurrection of our spiritual bodies we are taken up in the clouds before Christ, provided only that we pursue peace with good will while we are on earth.

From a Christmas Homily of St. Augustine of Hippo, trans. T.C. Lawler, *ACW 15*, p. 117.

5. The Virgin Mary: The Pride and Glory of Womankind

It is the Virgin's festival that summons us today to words of praise. This is a feast that has blessings to bestow on those who assemble to keep it. She who has assembled us here is the holy Mary; the untarnished vessel of virginity; the spiritual paradise of the second Adam; the workshop of the union of the [two] natures; the marketplace of the contract of salvation; the bride-chamber where the Word took the flesh in marriage; the living, human bush, which the fire of a divine childbirth did not consume [see Exodus 3:2]; the veritable swift cloud that carried into her body him who sits on the cherubim [Isaiah 19:1]; the purest fleece full of heavenly rain [Judges 6:37-38], whereby the shepherd clothed himself with the sheep; handmaid and mother, maiden and heaven, only bridge to human kind; the awesome loom of salvation on which the robe of the union was mysteriously woven [John 19:23]; whose weaver was the Holy Spirit, the workman the power that overshadowed from on high [see Luke 1:35], the wool the ancient fleece of Adam, the fabric the unsullied flesh of a virgin, the shuttle the immeasurable grace of him who wove it, and the craftsman the Word who entered her ear.

Who ever saw, who ever heard of God in his infinity dwelling in a womb? Heaven cannot contain him, yet a womb did not constrict him. He was born of woman, God but not solely God, man but not merely man. By his birth what once was the door of sin was made the gate of salvation. Through ears that disobeyed, the serpent poured in his poison; through ears that obeyed, the Word entered to form a living temple. In the first case it was Cain, the first pupil of sin, who emerged; in the second it was Christ, the redeemer of the race, who sprouted unsown into life.

St. Proclus of Constantinople (died 446), *Sermon 1, On Mary*, delivered in the cathedral of Hagia Sophia, either on the Sunday before Christmas or on December 26 of 428; trans. by Maurice Wiles and Mark Santer, *Documents in Early Christian Thought* (Cambridge University Press, 1977), pp. 61-62.

6. "A child has been born for us, a son given to us" (Isaiah 9:6).

    For us, I repeat, not for himself. He who was born of the Father before all ages was of more noble birth and had no need to be born in time of a mother. And he was not even born for the angels. They had him great among them and had no need of a little child. He was born for us, therefore, and given to us because we need him. Now that he has been born and given to us, let us accomplish the purpose of this birth and this donation. He came for our good, let us use him to our good, let us work out our salvation from the Savior. Look, a little child is put in our midst. ... Let us make every effort to become like this little child. Because he is meek and humble of heart, let us learn from him, lest he who is great, even God, should have been made a little man for nothing, lest he should have died to no purpose, and have been crucified in vain. Let us learn his humility, imitate his gentleness, embrace his love, share his sufferings, be washed in his blood. Let us offer him the propitiation for our sins because for this he was born and given for us. Let us offer him up in the sight of the Father, offer him too to his own, for the Father did not spare his own Son but gave him up for us all. And the Son emptied himself, taking the form of a slave (Philippians 2:7). He freely poured out his soul in death and was numbered with brigands and he bore the sins of many and interceded for transgressors that they might not perish. How can they perish whom the Son prayed might not perish, and for whose life the Father gave up his Son in death?

St. Bernard of Clairvaux (1090–1153), *Homilies in Praise of the Blessed Virgin Mary*, Homily 3, 14 (Kalamazoo, MI: Cistercian Publications, 1993), p. 44.

Readings for Assumptiontide

(These Readings are used from February 3 until Shrove Tuesday; and from the Monday after Pentecost until Advent):

Scripture Readings from the four gospels	Matthew 3-25
(excluding the stories of Jesus' birth	Mark 1-13
and his passion, death, and resurrection)	Luke 3-21
	John 1-11

Pause for meditation after the first reading.

Second Readings from the Fathers and other spiritual writers:

1. On the Dormition and Assumption of Mary
    The prophets proclaim you. The angels serve you, the apostles revere you, the virginal mouthpiece of God [the Beloved Disciple] takes care of the ever-virgin who was Mother of God. Today the angels minister to you as you go home to your Son, joined by the souls of the just, of patriarchs and prophets and the Apostles are your escort. . . .

    O, see how the source of life is carried over into life, through the midst of death! See how she who overcame the defining limits of nature in her childbearing now gives way to those same limits, and

261

submits her unsullied body to death! It was only right for that body to "lay aside what is mortal and put on immortality" (1 Corinthians 15:5), since the Lord of nature himself did not refuse the test of death. He died in the flesh, and by that death destroyed death, bestowed incorruptibility on corrupt nature, and made death the source of resurrection. See how the Maker of all things receives into his own hands her holy soul, now separated from that tabernacle that received God. He rightly honors her who was by nature his handmaid, but who by his saving plan he made to be his mother, in the unfathomable ocean of his love for humanity. . . .

O lovely emigration, which was for you a migration to God! For even if this is granted by God to all who are inspired to serve him—and it is granted to them all, we believe—still there is an infinite difference between God's servants and his mother. But even though your holy and blessed soul was separated from your privileged, immaculate body, and your body was committed to burial, as custom demanded, still it did not remain in death, nor was it dissolved by corruption. . . . Your immaculate, complete, spotless body was not left on earth, but you have been transported to the royal dwelling-place of heaven as queen, as lady, as mistress, as Mother of God, as the one who truly gave God birth.

St. John of Damascus (ca. 675–ca. 749), *On the Dormition of the Holy Mother of God*, Homily 1, 9-10, 12; trans. Brian E. Daley, S.J., *On the Dormition of Mary* (Crestwood, NY: St. Vladimir's Seminary Press, 1998), pp. 194-195, 198.

2. On the Assumption of Mary

Today let there be one common feast for the dwellers in heaven and on earth, let human beings rejoice along with the angels, and let every tongue join in the chorus and sing "Hail!" to the Mother of God. Gabriel, after all, did this before us, he proclaimed the preface to this mystery, when the most brilliant moment of God's self-revelation, the divine formation of Jesus as one like us, too place by an unprecedented and indescribable act of God's providence, in the workshop of a virgin's nature. So we once again, must offer this gift of thanks and principal honor to the Queen of our race; it is right to say "Hail" to her, now that she is removed from our midst! She alone has made joy her possession, for all our sakes, and has put flight the sadness of our first mother.

"Let us blow the trumpet in Sion; let us take up psaltery and harp!" (Psalm 80:3LXX). Let us sing to the Mother of God—sing not a bridal song, but strike up a funeral melody. Someone . . . will no doubt want to ask, "Why do you recall Sion, you who sing the glory of this holy feast?" Not without purpose, I would say to him. My friend, I recalled holy Sion, for in that mountain we are introduced into the great mystery of the Mother of God. These marble slabs, laid out as a floor, resounded far and wide with the bending knees of her holy body. For this was her dwelling for the whole time of her presence on earth; there she obeyed the laws of nature, and reached the end of her life; there she escaped the Prince of darkness [at death], just as in giving birth she escaped the pains of motherhood. Her name is holy, her title divine; she is above all stain; she has filled heaven and earth with glory and grace by the greatness of her divine journey.

St. Andrew of Crete (ca. 660–740), *On the Dormition of Our Most Holy Lady the Mother of God,* homily 1, 1, trans. Brian E. Daley, S.J., *On the Dormition of Mary,* pp. 103-104.

3. On the Assumption of Mary

Today the glorious Virgin goes up into heaven, doubtlessly causing the citizens of heaven to rejoice even more extravagantly. She is the one whose word of greeting caused those who were still enclosed in their mother's wombs to leap for joy. If the soul of an unborn baby is overcome when Mary spoke, what great joy will there be for the inhabitants of heaven who are found worthy to hear her voice, see her face, and enjoy her blessed presence?

For ourselves, dear friends, why is her Assumption a solemn occasion, a source of joy and gladness? The whole universe is enlightened by the presence of Mary. Even the heavenly homeland is brilliant with the light from this virginal lamp. There is good cause, therefore, for thanksgiving and praise to resound on high. But for us, perhaps, her departure is more a cause for mourning than for celebration. If it is true that heaven exults at her presence should we not, therefore, lament her absence from this lower world? There is no cause for complaint. Here we have no abiding city; rather we are seeking that one at which the blessed Mary arrives today. If we are enrolled as citizens of that place, we must remember that even though we are in exile by the rivers of Babylon, nevertheless we still share in the heavenly rejoicing. We have a part in that celebration. This is so because the river that gives joy to God's city is so abundant that even here on earth we can experience something of its torrent.

Our Queen has gone ahead of us. She precedes us. . . . From our pilgrim state we have sent an advocate before us. She is both the mother of the Judge and the mother of mercy, and hence will deal efficaciously in pleading the cause of our salvation. This day the earth delivers a precious gift to heaven so that in the process of giving and receiving a happy and intimate bond of friendship might be achieved between human beings and God, between the earthly and the heavenly, between the lowest and the highest. She who went up to that place from which every good and perfect gift descends was the most sublime fruit of earth. Gone up on high, the blessed Virgin will also give gifts to human beings. She certainly will give, since she lacks neither the possibility nor the will. She is the Queen of heaven and she is merciful; she is, in fact, the mother of God's only-begotten Son. There is nothing that can add either to her power or to her kindness. To think otherwise would be to believe that God's Son does not honor his mother. It is to doubt that the heart of Mary, in which for nine months the God of love rested bodily, did not receive from him the power of love.

St. Bernard of Clairvaux (1090–1153), *Assumption Sermons*, #1, trans. Michael Casey, O.C.S.O., *Bernard of Clairvaux, Man, Monk, Mystic* (Kalamazoo, MI: Cistercian Publications, 1991), pp. 87-89.

4.   On the Assumption of Mary

Who has the capacity to reflect on how the glorious Queen of the world went forth? With what depth of feeling did the whole multitude of all the heavenly legions go out to meet her? How they sang as she was led to the throne of glory! There she was received by her Son with placid countenance and serene face and with many divine embraces. She was exalted above all creatures to an honor worthy of such a mother, a glory befitting such a Son. Her lips used to be covered with the happy kisses of a baby, as the virginal mother played with him on her lap. But these kisses, which she receives in blessed salutation from the mouth of the One who sits on the Father's right, are even happier. Now she ascends the throne of glory singing the wedding song: "Let him kiss me with the kiss of his mouth" (Song of Songs 1:1).

Who has the power to describe the begetting of Christ or the Assumption of Mary? Just as on earth she obtained more grace than others, so in heaven, an outstanding glory is hers. "Eyes cannot see nor ear hear nor has it entered into the human heart to conceive what God has prepared for those who love him" (1 Corinthians 2:9). How much more has he prepared for the one who brought him to birth and who certainly loved him more than anyone else. . . . [Let us meditate this text] so that not only will our feelings of devotion be aroused in commemorating the Virgin, but our behavior will be improved and we will make some progress in our way of life. All to the praise and glory of her Son, our Lord, who is blessed above all things forever.

St. Bernard of Clairvaux, as above, pp. 90-92.

5. Mary, Star of the Sea

Mary means "star of the sea," and is becoming to the Virgin Mother.... She is indeed that noble star risen out of Jacob (Numbers 24:17) whose beam enlightens this earthly globe. She it is whose brightness both twinkles in the highest heaven and pierces the pit of hell, and is shed upon earth, warming our hearts far more than our bodies, fostering virtue and cauterizing vice. She, I tell you, is that splendid and wondrous star suspended over this great wide sea, radiant with merit and brilliant with example. O you, whoever you are, who feel that in the tidal wave of this world you are nearer to being tossed about among the squalls and gales than on dry land, if you do not want to founder in the tempest, do not avert your eyes from the brightness of this star. When the wind of temptation blows up within you, when you strike upon the rock of tribulation, gaze up at this star, call out to Mary. Whether you are being tossed about by the waves of pride or ambition or slander or jealousy, gaze up at this star, call out to Mary. When rage or greed or fleshly desires are battering the skiff of your soul, gaze up at Mary. When the immensity of your sins weighs you down and you are bewildered by the loathsomeness of your conscience, when the terrifying thought of judgment appalls you and you begin to founder in the gulf of sadness and despair, think of Mary. In dangers, in hardships, in every doubt, think of Mary, call out to Mary. Keep her in your mouth, keep her in your heart. Follow the example of her life and you will obtain the favor of her prayer. Following her, you will never go astray. Asking her help, you will never despair. Keeping her in your thoughts, you will never wander away. With your hand in hers, you will never stumble. With her protecting, you will never be afraid. With her leading you, you will never tire. Her kindness will see you through to the end.

St. Bernard of Clairvaux (1090–1153), *Homilies in Praise of the Blessed Virgin Mary*, Homily 2 (Kalamazoo, MI: Cistercian Publications, 1993), pp. 30-31.

6. A Simple Humble Maiden

Our Lord showed me a spiritual sight of his familiar love. I saw that he is to us everything which is good and comforting for our help. He is our clothing, for he is that love that wraps and enfolds us, embraces us and guides us, surrounds us for his love, which is so tender that he may never desert us. And so in this sight I saw truly that he is everything which is good.

In this God brought our Lady to my understanding. I saw her spiritually in her bodily likeness, a simple, humble maiden, young in years, of the stature which she had when she conceived. Also God showed me part of the wisdom and truth of her soul, and in this I understood the reverent contemplation with which she beheld her God, marveling with great reverence that he was willing to be born of her who was a simple creature created by him. And this wisdom and truth, this knowledge of her Creator's greatness and of her own created littleness, made her say meekly to the angel Gabriel: Behold me here, God's handmaiden. In this sight I saw truly that she is greater, more worthy and more fulfilled, than everything else which God has created, and which is inferior to her. Above her is no created thing, except the blessed humanity of Christ.

Julian of Norwich (ca. 1342–1416), *Showings,* trans. Edmund Colledge, O.S.A. and James Walsh, S.J., Short Text, chap. 4 (New York: Paulist Press, 1978), pp. 130-131.

7. Mary: Spiritual Mother of the Christian Community

The disciple whom Jesus loved can say of Mary that she is the Mother of Jesus and also his mother; he realizes then the intimacy which unites him with Christ, his Lord and his Brother. Mary, the Mother of Jesus and his mother, is the person who is able to draw him closer to Christ, his Lord and his God. With him, she has been a witness of the last moments of the Crucifixion, she has heard the last words of

Jesus, and has received the Spirit which he has transmitted to the Church. Mary is therefore for him and, through him, for all the disciples and for the Church which gathers about them, a very close sign of the presence of the Lord, a spiritual mother in the Christian community, the most venerated of all the spiritual mothers found in the Church, the spiritual mother *par excellence* of the beloved and faithful disciple, of the brother of Jesus, which every Christian is called to be.

Immediately after the Ascension, we see, in the Acts of the Apostles [1:12-14] the group of the Eleven returning to Jerusalem and going into the Upper Room where they had habitually met with Christ. There they are to await the outpouring of the Spirit at Pentecost. "All these with one accord devoted themselves to prayer, together with the women, Mary, the mother of Jesus, and with his brothers" (Acts 1:14). Mary, the Mother of Jesus, is here integrated with the whole group of the disciples: the apostles, the women and the relatives of the Lord. With them, and in the midst of them, being of one heart and mind with them, she is assiduous in prayer, awaiting the great outpouring of the Holy Spirit which will open the missionary era of the Church. . . .

She appears like a widow of the ancient Church "who sets her hope in God and continues in supplication and prayer night and day" (1 Timothy 5:5). However, she is not alone; she has a son in the disciple whom Jesus loved; she is the spiritual mother *par excellence* in the midst of the faithful women who have followed Christ and who are always there. She is for the disciple, and for all the disciples, the type of Mother Church and the spiritual mother rediscovered in the Church. In the power of the Spirit, she will be able to transmit to the disciples and to the primitive Church all that she knew of Jesus, her beloved Son, and what she has so preciously guarded and pondered in her heart (Luke 2:19, 51). She will be a humble bearer of the gospel of her Son . . . in the manner of a discreet and loving mother, a human mother, the mother of the Son of God whom she has known better than anyone in the intimacy of his company, a spiritual mother of the disciples, to recall all that Christ said and did, and of whom she had been the faithful and attentive hearer. By her faith, her hope, her charity, and her prayers she will be a spiritual Mother of Mother Church, of whom she is the living and humble representative.

Max Thurian of Taize, *Mary, Mother of All Christians* (New York: Herder and Herder, 1964), pp. 170-171.

8. Mary, Mediatrix of All Graces

The absolutely unique "Yes" of the Blessed Virgin, which co-operated in determining the whole history of the world, is not a mere happening that has disappeared into the void of the past. It occurred as an event in a personal, spiritual history, by grace, and therefore it is—it is eternally. She still utters her eternal Amen, her eternal *Fiat.* Let it be so, Let it be done, to all that God willed, to the whole great ordered plan of redemption, in which we all find place, built up on the foundation which is Christ. She says Amen to it all, because she consented once and for all to Jesus Christ, and because that consent of hers has entered eternity. When God looks upon the one community of the redeemed, and wills each with all the others, and because he wills the others, he also looks upon this eternal Yes of the Blessed Virgin, the Yes on which he willed, in this order of creation, the salvation of us all, quite directly and absolutely once and for all, to depend. God, therefore, wills our salvation too, in this view of his of Mary as she is in eternal life. When he looks upon her, he sees in her too only the grace of the Word made flesh, and he wills us on her account only because he loves her as the mother of his Son. But because God gives what is his sheer grace to its recipient in such a way that it is truly possessed as the recipient's own, though it still continues inalienably to belong to God and to Christ, this special and individual grace of God is only really recognized and praised when those to whom it is given are aware of it. Such praise does not diminish, but increases the glory of the utter grace of the one Mediator.

For that reason, therefore, we can truly say of Mary, on account of what she did in the history of redemption, she is the intercessor for all of us, the mediatrix of all graces.

Karl Rahner, S.J., Mary, *Mother of the Lord* (New York: Herder and Herder, 1963), pp. 100-101.

9. The Blessed Virgin Mary: The Second Vatican Council (1962-65)

    Mary is acknowledged as both the Mother of God and Mother of the Redeemer. Because of this, she has a place of honor both in the Church and in heaven. She has a unique relationship with God and a special relationship to the Church. And although she is unlike us in these ways, she is also like us in the most fundamental aspects of her nature: She is in need of salvation, not because of any sin, but simply because she is human. Mary does not stand above Christ, but stands with all of us who need a savior. What a remarkable relationship this is! Jesus depended on Mary for the things of this earth. Mary depended on Jesus for the things of heaven!

This, of course, means that Mary is a member of the Church and an excellent example of faith and charity. We Catholics, therefore, honor her with childlike affection.

From the very beginning of time, God had something important planned for Mary. The place of Mary in the plan of salvation is even foretold in the writings of Isaiah, a Hebrew prophet: "A virgin shall give birth to a son and the nations will call him Emmanuel, 'God with us.'" Yet though she was part of God's plan, Mary was free to say yes or no to God. Her role was not forced upon her.

Rather God had great things in store for Mary, and she freely chose to accept them. That willingness on her part to serve is an essential part of the working out of holiness, the fight against sin in the world, and the coming of the Holy Spirit. It is no wonder that the earliest members of the Church quickly developed a sense of awe at Mary's place and role! We believe God willed this: that Mary's acceptance of the angel's call would precede the conception of Jesus and that Mary, a virgin forever, would give birth to Emmanuel, Jesus Christ.

This is often seen as the reversal of the story of Adam and Eve: By the actions of one man and one woman, sin and suffering entered the world and our relationship with God was put in turmoil. Jesus Christ, the new Adam, restored grace to the world, and Mary participated in this through her loving cooperation with God.

The Second Vatican Council, *Constitution on the Church* (November 21, 1964), chapter 8, 60-69, paraphrased by Bill Huebsch, *Vatican II in Plain English* (Allen, TX: Thomas More, 1996), pp. 61-68.

10. On Mary: The Second Vatican Council, contd.

The New Testament has many examples of the unfolding of this plan to save the world: Elizabeth greeted Mary and called her "blessed," causing the infant to leap within her. Jesus' birth left Mary fresh and fulfilled. The spontaneous worship of the shepherds, the glorious visit of the magi, the presentation in the temple, the prophetic words of Simeon, and, finally, Jesus being lost in the temple, and three days later found, all these were part of Mary's parental devotion and work, and all of them complete the unfolding story of the Incarnation. Indeed, in Jesus' ministry, Mary was also present at key moments. From Cana to the cross, Mary was present: faithful mother, faithful daughter of God.

After Jesus' death, Mary remained present: she persevered in prayer and waited in faith with the apostles and other women who had also known Jesus. And we believe that Mary is now as close to Jesus as ever, present with God in heaven.

The Second Vatican Council, as above.

11. On Mary: The Second Vatican Council

Christ is the one Mediator between God and humanity. Because of the Holy Spirit, we have a direct friendship with Jesus, who can bring us into an intimate relationship with God. Our devotion to Mary must never diminish that. But since she played such a pivotal role in the life and work of Christ, we now realize that she is the first to receive the grace we also seek. And even though Mary's place is subordinate to Christ's, nonetheless, we still understand her to be a great helper on our way to holiness. By her belief and obedience and through the work of the Holy Spirit, she gave birth to Jesus and raised him with Joseph. Her faith remained strong: Even though she must have faced temptations just like Adam and Eve, and just like Jesus, she listened instead to God's message. Since Mary is the mother of Jesus and we are sisters and brothers of Jesus, we can call Mary our mother as well. How appropriate this is, and how privileged we are to have such a mother, one who is eternally attentive to our struggles and always ready to nurture us spiritually!

The Second Vatican Council, as above.

12. On Mary: The Second Vatican Council
The Church takes Mary as its example and always tries to imitate her life and always seeks to give birth to the presence of Christ in the world. Hence, the Church is also a mother to the faithful, bearing Christ for them, gently guiding them in life to an entire faith, a firm hope, and a sincere charity.

Therefore the faithful now turn their eyes to Mary as the model of virtue. By meditating on her, we grow more and more like her Son and enter more intimately into the mystery of the Incarnation. We honor Mary and have a piety toward her so that we can better know Christ and the whole world can be more open to receiving the grace of Christ. There is absolutely no other reason for our devotion to Mary.

Mary's place is with God in heaven. This gives us great hope of what we ourselves can look forward to. And so with great longing and heartfelt trust, we bring our prayers to Mary and ask her to pray for us. We know that she desires exactly what God desires and what we really want: That in the end all will be restored in Christ, and everyone will live in peace with God and with one another. Then we will truly know what it means to be the people of God. Then we will fully understand that Christ is the Light of the Nations. *Lumen Gentium*!

The Second Vatican Council, as above.

13. Mary and the Second Coming of Christ

It is through the Holy Virgin that Jesus Christ came into the world to begin with, and it is also through her that he will reign in the world. . . .

I say with the saints: Mary is the terrestrial paradise of the New Adam, where he was incarnate by the operation of the Holy Spirit to work incomprehensible miracles; she is the great, divine world of God where there are ineffable beauties and treasures. She is the magnificence of the Most High where he has hidden, as if in his own breast, his only Son.

Until now, the divine Mary has been unknown, and this is one of the reasons why Jesus Christ is hardly known as he should be. If then—as is certain—the knowledge and reign of Jesus Christ arrive in this world, it will be a necessary consequence of the knowledge and reign of the Holy Virgin, who birthed him into this world the first time and will make him burst out everywhere the second. . . .

Mary has produced, with the Holy Spirit, the greatest thing that has ever been—or will ever be—the God-Man, and she will produce the greatest things that shall be in these last times. The formation and education of the heroic saints that will come at the end of the world are reserved for her. Only this singular and miraculous Virgin can produce, in union with the Holy Spirit, singular and extraordinary things. . . .

Mary is the dawn that precedes and reveals the Sun of Justice. . . . The difference between the first and the second coming of Jesus will be that the first was secret and hidden, the second will be glorious and dazzling; both will be perfect, because both will come through Mary. This is a great and holy mystery.

St. Louis-Marie Grignion de Montfort (1673–1716), *True Devotion to the Blessed Virgin*, trans. Andrew Harvey, *Teachings of the Christian Mystics* (Boston: Shambhala, 1998), pp. 142-144.

Readings for the Season of Lent
(See the Table of Feasts, page 30)

Bible Readings for the Season of Lent:

(read in short selections)

"The Passion Gospels"	Matthew 21–27
	Mark 9–15
	Luke 19–23
	John 11–19
The Sermon on the Mount	Matthew 5–7
	Luke 6:17–46

The Letter of Paul to the Romans

Pause for meditation after the first reading.

Second Readings from the Fathers and other spiritual writers:

1. Mary at the Cross
    Jesus' mother was standing near the cross and, even though others fled, she stood there undaunted. Notice how the mother of Jesus knew how to combine womanly reserve with fearless courage. She fixed her loving eyes on the wounds of her Son by which she knew the world would be redeemed. This noble mother continued to watch the spectacle of

her dying Son without fear of the executioners. As long as her Son was hanging on the cross, his mother insisted on facing his persecutors.

Homily of St. Ambrose, Bishop of Milan (ca. 339–397), *On Virgins,* trans. WGS.

2. The Compassion of Mary

I saw part of the compassion of our Lady, St. Mary, for Christ and she were so united in love that the greatness of her love was the cause of the greatness of her pain. For her pain surpassed that of all others, as much as she loved him more than all others. And so all his disciples and all his true lovers suffered greater pains than they did at the death of their own bodies. For I am sure, by my own experience, that the least of them loved him more than they loved themselves. And here I saw a great unity between Christ and us; for when he was in pain we were in pain, and all creatures able to suffer pain suffered with him. And for those who did not know him, their pain was that of all creation, sun and moon ceased to serve men, and so they were all abandoned in sorrow at that time. So those who loved him suffered pain for their love, and those who did not love him suffered pain because the comfort of all creation failed them.

Julian of Norwich, *Showings* (Short text), chap. 10, ed. and trans. Edmund Colledge, O.S.A. and James Walsh, S.J. (New York: Paulist Press, 1978), pp. 142–143.

3. Mary's Universal Motherhood

What died in Mary's heart on the eve of Christ's passion was the merely human love she still had for Christ as her human son; what was born in her heart on the day he rose was her universal motherhood. For this to happen, it is quite true to say that something in her heart had to die: it was the end of a great happiness, of the thirty-three years she had lived with God made man. That is why when Christ, indicating John, said to her: "Woman, behold your son" (John 19:26), a sword pierced deep into her heart, it was the end of a marvelous reality. At that moment, she went beyond the love concentrated on the humanity of Jesus, she opened her heart wide enough to include the whole of humanity. This could only be done by death, by that death of the heart, by as deep a suffering in her heart as our Lord had in his body; for this too, this growth of charity, this outgoing of love that was to embrace the world, could only come about through death.

Jean Danielou, S.J., *The Advent of Salvation* (New York: Paulist Press, 1962), p. 117.

4. Mary's Martyrdom

The account of the Virgin's martyrdom appears both in the prophecy of Simeon and in the story of the Lord's passion. "This child is destined to be a sign that will be contradicted," old Simeon said of the child Jesus; "And a sword will pierce your own soul too," he said to Mary. Yes, Blessed Mother, the sword did pierce your soul, for only by passing through your soul could it penetrate the body of your Son. And when this Jesus of yours had surrendered his spirit to his Father and the cruel spear which opened his side could not touch his soul any more, it still pierced yours. His soul was no longer there but yours could not be wrenched away. The sword of sorrow did indeed pass through your soul so that we may truly call you more than martyr; the love which made you suffer far exceeded any bodily pain. Was not that word of his—"Woman, here is your son"—sharper than any sword, reaching as it did to the division of soul and spirit? What an exchange! John for Jesus, the servant for the Lord, the disciple for the Master, the son of Zebedee for the Son of God, a mere man for the true God. How sharply must the sound of those words have pierced your loving soul when the mere memory of them wrings our stony, our iron hearts with sorrow. We should not be surprised that Mary is called a martyr in spirit. The only people to be surprised at such an expression are those who do not recall Paul's words mentioning among the greater sins of the Gentiles that they were "without affection." Such lack of affection was not characteristic of Mary's heart—and may it not be of ours! Perhaps someone will say: Didn't she know beforehand that he was going to die? Certainly she did! Didn't she expect that he would quickly rise from the dead? Yes, faithfully! Did she still lament his crucifixion? Yes, bitterly! How can we be more astonished at Mary in her compassion that at Mary's Son in his passion? He could die the death of the body; could she not die with him in spirit? In Jesus, love was the reason, a love greater than any other; in Mary, too, love was the explanation, a love that could not be duplicated.

Sermon of St. Bernard, Abbot of Clairvaux (1090–1153), *On the Twelve Stars*, trans. WGS.

5. Christ's Last Will and Testament

Mary, the mother of the Lord, stood by the cross of her Son. Only St. John the Evangelist teaches us this. The other evangelists wrote that during the passion of the Lord the world shook, the sky was shrouded in darkness, the sun disappeared, the criminal was admitted into paradise after a devout confession. John taught what the other gospel writers did not teach: how hanging on the cross, Jesus called out to his mother. Now that Jesus, in the midst of his sufferings, thought of his mother is considered more important than his gift of paradise to the repentant felon. If the forgiveness of the criminal was a virtuous act, it was an even greater sign of devotion that the Son should honor his mother with such affection. "Here," he says to Mary, "here is your son"; to the disciple, "Here is your mother." From the cross Christ made this last will and testament and was dutiful to both his mother and his beloved disciple. The Lord made a will that was both public and private and this will was signed by the disciple whom he loved, a witness worthy of such a testator. It was a fine will, leaving not money but life eternal; written not in ink but by the Spirit of the living God.

St. Ambrose, Bishop of Milan (ca. 339–397), *Epistle 25 to the Church of Vercelli*, trans. WGS.

6. Mary's Sword of Sorrow

What tongue can tell, what intellect grasp the heavy weight of your desolation, blessed Virgin? You were present at all these events, standing close by and participating in them in every way. This blessed and most holy flesh—which you so chastely conceived, so sweetly nourished and fed with your milk, which you so often held on your lap, and kissed with your lips—you actually gazed upon with your bodily eyes now torn by the blows of the scourges, now pierced by the points of the thorns, now struck by the reed, now beaten by hands and fists, now pierced by nails and fixed to the wood of the cross, now torn by its own weight as it hung there, now mocked in every way, finally made to drink gall and vinegar. But with the eye of your mind you saw that divine soul filled with the gall of every form of bitterness, now groaning in spirit, now quaking with fear, now wearied, now in agony, now in anxiety, now in confusion, now oppressed by sadness and sorrow, partly because of his most sensitive response to bodily pain, partly because of his most fervent zeal for the divine honor taken away by sin, partly because of his pity poured out upon wretched human beings, partly because of his compassion for you, his most sweet mother, as the sword pierced the depths of your heart, when with devoted eyes he looked upon you standing before him and spoke to you these loving words: "Woman, behold your son," (John 19:26) in order to console in its trials your soul, which he knew had been more deeply pierced by a sword of compassion than if you had suffered in your body.

St. Bonaventure, O.F.M. (1217–1274), trans. Ewert Cousins, *Bonaventure* (New York: Paulist Press, 1978), pp. 152-153.

Readings for the Season of Easter (See the Table of Feasts, page 30)

Bible Readings for the Season of Easter:

(read in short selections)

Matthew 28:1-20
Mark 16
Luke 24
John 20 & 21
1 Corinthians 15:1-58
The Acts of the Apostles

Pause for meditation after the first reading.

Second Readings from the Fathers and other spiritual writers:

1. The Day of Days

   Let us celebrate this greatest and most shining feast, on which the Lord has risen from the dead. Let us celebrate it with joy, and in equal measure with devotion. For the Lord has risen, and together with him he has raised the whole world. He has risen, because he has broken the bonds of death.

St. John Chrysostom (ca. 347–407), *Homily for Easter Sunday*, PG 50, 437; trans. M.F. Toal, *Sunday Sermons of the Great Fathers* (Swedesboro, NJ: Preservation Press, 1996), vol. 2.

2. Genuine Birth, Death, and Resurrection

   Great was the mercy of God the Father: he sent the creative Word, who, when he came to save us, put himself in our position, and in the same situation in which we lost life; and he loosed the prison-bonds, and his light appeared and dispelled the darkness in the prison, and he sanctified our birth and abolished death, loosing those same bonds by which we were held. And he showed forth the resurrection, becoming "the first born from the dead" (Colossians 1:18), and raised in himself prostrate man, being lifted up to the heights of heaven, at the right hand of the glory of the Father, as God promised through the prophet, saying: "I will raise up the booth of David that is fallen" (Amos 9:11), that is, the body sprung from David; and this was in truth accomplished by our Lord Jesus Christ, in the triumph of our redemption, that he raised us in truth, setting us free to the Father. And if anyone accept not his virgin birth, how shall he accept his resurrection from the dead?

St. Irenaeus of Lyons (ca. 130–ca. 200), *Proof of the Apostolic Preaching, 39*, [*Ancient Christian Writers 15*], trans. Joseph P. Smith, S.J. (New York: Newman Press, 1952), pp. 71-72.

3. The Eve-Mary Parallel

   "Mary and the other Mary came to see the tomb" (Matthew 28:1).

She who had taken perfidy away from paradise hurries to take faith from the tomb; she, who had snatched death from the hands of life, hastens to snatch life from the hands of death. "Mary came." The name is that of the Mother of Christ; that is, the Mother came, the woman came, so that she who had become the mother of the dying might become now the mother of the living, and so that what had been written might be fulfilled: "She was the mother of all the living" (Genesis 3:20).

St. Peter Chrysologus (ca. 380–ca. 450), *Sermon 74, 3*, trans. Thomas Buffer in Luigi Gambero, S.M., *Mary and the Fathers of the Church* (San Francisco: Ignatius Press, 1999), p. 299.

4.   Appearances of the Risen Christ

When the third day dawned of the Lord's sacred repose in the tomb, which in the cycle of the weeks is both the eighth and the first, Christ, *the power and wisdom of God* (1 Cor. 1:24), with the author of death lying prostrate, conquered even death itself and opened to us access to eternity, when he raised himself from the dead by his divine power in order to make known to us the paths of life (Psalm 15:11). Then there was a great earthquake; for an angel of the Lord came down from heaven, with raiment like snow and his countenance like lightning (Matt. 28:2-3). He appeared attractive to the devout and severe to the wicked; for he terrified the cruel soldiers and comforted the timid women, to whom the Lord himself first appeared after rising because their intense devotion so merited. Then he was seen by Peter, then by the disciples going to Emmaus, then by all the apostles, except Thomas. Later he presented himself to be touched by Thomas, who proclaimed his faith: My Lord and my God! (John 20:28). And thus during forty days he appeared in many ways to his disciples, both eating and drinking with them; and he enlightened our faith with proofs and lifted up our hope with promises so as finally to enkindle our love with gifts from heaven.

St. Bonaventure, O.F.M. (1217–1274), *The Tree of Life*, #34, trans. Ewert Cousins, *Bonaventure* (New York: Paulist Press, 1978), pp. 159-160.

5. To Jesus Through Mary
    Very merrily and gladly, our Lord looked into his side, and he gazed and said this: See how I loved you; as if he had said: my child, if you cannot look at my divinity, see here how I suffered my side to be opened and my heart to be split in two and to send out blood and water, all that was in it; and this is a delight to me, and I wish it to be so for you.

    Our Lord showed us this to make us glad and merry. And with the same joyful appearance he looked down on his right, and brought to my mind where our Lady stood at the time of his Passion, and he said: Do you wish to see her? And I answered and said: Yes, good Lord, great thanks, if it be your will.

Often times I had prayed for this, and I expected to see her in a bodily likeness; but I did not see her so. And Jesus, saying this, showed me a spiritual vision of her. Just as before I had seen her small and simple, now he showed her high and noble and glorious and more pleasing to him than all creatures. And so he wishes it to be known that all who take delight in him should take delight in her, and in the delight that he has in her and she in him. And when Jesus said: Do you wish to see her? it seemed to me that I had the greatest delight that he could have given me in this spiritual vision of her which he gave me. For our Lord showed me no particular person except our Lady, St. Mary, and he showed her to me on three occasions. The first was as she conceived, the second was as she had been in her sorrow under the Cross, and the third as she is now, in delight, honor and joy.

And after this our Lord showed himself to me, and he appeared to me more glorified than I had seen him before, and in this I was taught that every contemplative soul to whom it is given to look and to seek will see Mary and pass on to God through contemplation.

Julian of Norwich (1342–ca. 1423), *Showings*, chap. 13 (Short text), ed. and trans. Edmund Colledge, O.S.A. and James Walsh, S.J. (New York: Paulist Press, 1978), pp. 146-147.

6. Mary at the Font

   Our rebirth in baptism is symbolized in the birth which, overshadowed by the Spirit, gave us the Redeemer born of the Virgin. If then the Church as the Mystical Body of Christ is ever being born again in the sacrament of baptism, if "in one Spirit we are all baptized into one body . . . and in one Spirit we have all been made to drink" (1 Corinthians 12:13), then baptism is for ever the continuation of the birth of God made man, born of the Virgin, conceived by the Spirit. This is the old theology of baptism, which will perhaps enable us to understand more deeply the beginning of grace in our souls, with the attendant figures of the mother of Jesus and our mother the Church. . . .

   Let us recall a text of Irenaeus: "How was humanity to escape this birth into death, unless born again through faith, by that new birth from the Virgin, the sign of salvation that is God's wonderful and unmistakable gift?" (*Against Heresies* IV, 33, 4; PG 7, 1074). These words, from a theologian who was the heir of St. John, of course apply first to the Virgin Mary, but in so far as she is a type of the Church, the mother of the Mystical Body, they also apply to the birth of the children of salvation in baptism.

Mary is therefore in a real sense the beginning of our baptismal grace, so that Irenaeus can state it simply: "Chastely Christ opened the chaste womb, so that thence human beings might similarly be reborn" (*Against Heresies* IV, 33, 11; PG 7, 1080). And it is not a different idea, but a continuation of the same symbolic relationship of Mary to the Church, when Ambrose says: "Christ alone opened the silent, immaculate and fruitful womb of the holy Church for the birth of the people of God" (*Commentary on Luke* 2, 57; PL 15, 1573). The beginning is with Mary: the fulfillment with baptism, which draws forth the Body of Christ from the womb of the virgin mother, which is the Church. . . . Augustine said the same thing in his own way: "God was born of a woman, so that we could be born again of God. He needed a mother on earth, a father he had in heaven. . . . He, through whom all things were made, was born of God from all eternity: but he was born of a woman, that he might make all things new" (*Treatise on John* 2, 15; PL 35, 1395).

The womb of Mary is the womb of the Church. Still to be seen in that ancient prototype of all baptisteries at the Lateran is the inscription carved in marble, which proclaims in the poetry of the fifth century the Marian mystery of the Church's motherhood through baptism:

The Church, Virgin-Mother, brings forth from the River. The children she conceived by the breath of God. Text in Diehl, *Inscriptiones latinae christianae veteres* (Rome, 1926).

The author of these lines was none the less than Leo the Great, who composed them when he was the deacon of Pope Sixtus III. . . . Leo never tired of reminding his hearers of the connection of the feast with the grace of baptism. . . . The power in baptism is foreshadowed in the power that overshadowed the Virgin: at every baptismal font the Church is there as mother, and the mother of Jesus is there.

Hugo Rahner, *Our Lady and the Church* (New York: Pantheon Press, 1961), pp. 59-62.

7. Our Lady of Mercy

O Blessed Virgin, if there are any who remember having been left unsatisfied after having called upon you in time of trouble, let them be silent about your kindness. We who are your familiar servants are happy about all your virtues but especially about this one. We acclaim your virginity, we admire your humility, but it is your mercy that we poor people find most pleasing. We attach ourselves to your mercy with special love. We remember it especially often and we appeal to it with greater urgency. It was your mercy that brought about the repair of the whole world and which pleads for the salvation of all human beings. For it is clear that she was concerned with the whole race since it was said to her: "Do not fear, O Mary, for you have found grace."

O Blessed Lady, who is able to comprehend the length and the breadth, the height and the depth of your mercy? It is long because it comes to the help of all who call upon you, even to the last day. It is broad because it fills the whole earthly sphere so that earth is full of your kindness also. It is high because it accomplishes the restoration of the heavenly city and it is deep because it obtains redemption "for those who sit in darkness and in the shadow of death." Because of you heaven is filled and hell is emptied, the ruins of the heavenly Jerusalem are rebuilt and the life that was lost is given to the poor who await it. Your love is powerful and yet motherly, it is able to feel compassion and, at the same time, it is able to provide abundant help. In both ways you enrich us.

Let your motherliness which has found favor with God be known to the world by obtaining, through your prayers, pardon for sin, healing for sickness, consolation for those in trouble, help for those in danger, and liberation for the saints.

St. Bernard of Clairvaux (1090–1153), *Man, Monk, Mystic*, text selected and translated by Michael Casey, O.C.S.O. (Kalamazoo, MI: Cistercian Publications, 1990), pp. 93-94.

The Litanies

of the Blessed

Virgin Mary

Litanies are an ancient form of prayer that were first created for use in the Eucharist and in the Liturgy of the Hours. In the Middle Ages they also came to be used in processions, in prayers of intercession before the Blessed Sacrament and, later on, at the end of the Rosary. The Marian litanies are particularly designed for intercessory prayer and are often used during a triduum or a novena to our Lady. In this book they are used at Evening Prayer but may, of course, be used separately as a devotion in themselves.

First Litany of Our Lady (Loreto)

Lord, have mercy.	—Lord, have mercy.
Christ, have mercy.	—Christ, have mercy.
Lord, have mercy.	—Lord, have mercy.

God our Father in heaven,	—Have mercy on us.
God the Son, Redeemer of the world,	—Have mercy on us.
God the Holy Spirit,	—Have mercy on us.
Holy Trinity, one God,	—Have mercy on us.

Holy Mary,	—Pray for us.
Holy Mother of God,	
Most honored of virgins,	

Mother of Christ,
Mother of the Church,
Mother of divine grace,

Mother most pure,
Mother of chaste love,
Mother and virgin,
Sinless Mother,
Dearest of mothers,
Model of motherhood,
Mother of good counsel,
Mother of our Creator,
Mother of our Savior,

Virgin most wise,
Virgin rightly praised,
Virgin rightly renowned,
Virgin most powerful,
Virgin gentle in mercy,
Faithful virgin,
Mirror of justice,
Throne of wisdom,
Cause of our joy,

Shrine of the Spirit,
Glory of Israel,
Vessel of selfless devotion,
Mystical rose,
Tower of David,
Tower of ivory,
House of gold,
Ark of the covenant,

Gate of heaven,
Morning Star,
Health of the sick,
Refuge of sinners,
Comfort of the troubled,
Help of Christians,

Queen of angels,
Queen of patriarchs and prophets,
Queen of apostles and martyrs,
Queen of confessors and virgins,
Queen of all saints,
Queen conceived in grace,
Queen raised up to glory,
Queen of the rosary,
Queen of peace,

Lamb of God, you take away the sins of the world,
—Have mercy on us.
Lamb of God, you take away the sins of the world,
—Have mercy on us.
Lamb of God, you take away the sins of the world,
—Have mercy on us.

Pause for spontaneous prayers of intercession.

Pray for us, holy Mother of God,
—That we may become worthy of the promises of
Christ.

Let us pray:
Eternal God,
let your people enjoy constant health in mind and
　　body.
Through the intercession of the Virgin Mary
free us from the sorrows of this life
and lead us to happiness in the life to come.
Grant this through Christ our Lord.
—Amen.

This Marian litany contains invocations that date back to the 12th
century. It was recorded in its present form (apart from a few additions
made by recent popes) at the shrine of Loreto in 1558 and approved by
Pope Sixtus V (1585–1590). This translation is taken from *A Book of
Prayers*, International Commission on English in the Liturgy, © 1982.

Second Litany of Our Lady

Lord, have mercy	—Lord, have mercy.
Christ, have mercy	—Christ, have mercy.
Lord, have mercy	—Lord, have mercy.
God our Father in heaven	—Have mercy on us.
God the Son,	
Redeemer of the world	—Have mercy on us.
God the Holy Spirit	—Have mercy on us.
Holy Trinity, one God	—Have mercy on us.
Holy Mary	—Pray for us.
Holy Mother of God	—Pray for us.
Most honored of virgins	—Pray for us.

Chosen daughter of the Father
Mother of Christ the King
Glory of the Holy Spirit

Virgin daughter of Zion
Virgin poor and humble
Virgin gentle and obedient

Handmaid of the Lord
Mother of the Lord
Helper of the Redeemer

Full of grace
Fountain of beauty
Model of virtue

Finest fruit of the redemption
Perfect disciple of Christ
Untarnished image of the Church

Woman transformed
Woman clothed with the sun
Woman crowned with stars

Gentle lady
Gracious lady
Our Lady

Joy of Israel
Splendor of the Church
Pride of the human race

Advocate of peace
Minister of holiness
Champion of God's people

Queen of love
Queen of mercy
Queen of peace

Queen of angels
Queen of patriarchs and prophets
Queen of apostles and martyrs
Queen of confessors and virgins

Queen of all saints
Queen conceived without original sin
Queen assumed into heaven

Queen of all the earth
Queen of heaven
Queen of the universe

Lamb of God, you take away the sins of the world,
—spare us, O Lord.
Lamb of God, you take away the sins of the world,
—hear us, O Lord.
Lamb of God, you take away the sins of the world,
—have mercy on us.

Pause for spontaneous prayers of intercession.

Pray for us, O glorious Mother of the Lord.
—That we may become worthy of the promises of Christ.

Let us pray:
God of mercy,
listen to the prayers of your servants
who have honored your handmaid Mary as mother
     and queen.
Grant that by your grace
we may serve you and our neighbor on earth
and be welcomed into your eternal kingdom.
We ask this through Christ our Lord.
—Amen.

A Book of Prayers (Washington, D.C.: I.C.E.L., 1987).

Litany of Mary of Nazareth

Glory to you, God our Creator . . .
Breathe into us new life, new meaning.
Glory to you, God our Savior . . .
Lead us in the way of peace and justice.
Glory to you, healing Spirit . . .
Transform us to empower others.

Mary, wellspring of peace—be our guide.
Model of strength
Model of gentleness
Model of trust

Model of courage
Model of patience
Model of risk
Model of openness
Model of perseverance

Model of the liberator—pray for us.
Mother of the homeless
Mother of the dying
Mother of the nonviolent
Widowed mother
Unwed mother
Mother of a political prisoner
Mother of the condemned
Mother of the executed criminal

Oppressed woman—lead us to life.
Liberator of the oppressed
Marginalized woman
Comforter of the afflicted
Cause of our joy
Sign of contradiction
Breaker of bondage
Political refugee
Seeker of sanctuary
First Disciple
Sharer in Christ's passion
Seeker of God's will
Witness to Christ's resurrection

Woman of mercy—empower us.
Woman of faith
Woman of contemplation
Woman of vision
Woman of wisdom and understanding
Woman of grace and truth
Woman, pregnant with hope
Woman, centered in God.

Closing Prayer

Mary, Queen of Peace,
we entrust our lives to you,
Shelter us from war, hatred, and oppression.
Teach us
to live in peace,
to educate ourselves for peace.
Inspire us to act justly,
to revere all God has made.
Root peace firmly in our hearts and in our world.
Amen.

Pax Christi USA

Litany of St. Joseph, Spouse of Mary

Lord, have mercy.	—Lord, have mercy.
Christ, have mercy.	—Christ have mercy.
Lord, have mercy.	—Lord, have mercy.

God our Father in heaven, —Have mercy on us.
God the Son, Redeemer
of the world, —Have mercy on us.
God the Holy Spirit, —Have mercy on us.
Holy Trinity, one God, —Have mercy on us.

Holy Mary, —Pray for us.
St. Joseph, —Pray for us.
Noble son of the House of David,
Light of patriarchs,
Husband of the Mother of God,
Guardian of the Virgin,
Foster-father of the Son of God,
Faithful guardian of Christ,
Head of the holy family,

Joseph, chaste and just,
Joseph, prudent and brave,
Joseph, obedient and loyal,
Pattern of patience,
Lover of poverty,
Model of workers,
Example to parents,
Guardian of virgins,
Pillar of family life,
Comfort of the troubled,
Hope of the sick,
Patron of the dying,

Terror of evil spirits,
Protector of the Church.

Lamb of God, you take away the sins of the world,
—Have mercy on us.
Lamb of God, you take away the sins of the world,
—Have mercy on us.
Lamb of God, you take away the sins of the world,
—Have mercy on us.

Pause for spontaneous prayers.

God made him master of his household,
—And put him in charge of all that he owned.

Let us pray:
Almighty God,
in your infinite wisdom and love
you chose Joseph to be the husband of Mary,
the mother of your Son.
As we enjoy his protection on earth
may we have the help of his prayers in heaven.
We ask this through Christ our Lord.
—Amen.

This litany was approved for devotional use by St. Pius X (1903–1914).

The Memorare

Remember, most loving Virgin Mary,
never was it heard
that anyone who turned to you for help
was left unaided.

Inspired by this confidence,
though burdened by my sins,
I run to your protection
for you are my mother.

Mother of the Word of God,
do not despise my words of pleading
but be merciful and hear my prayer.

An abbreviation of a fifteenth-century prayer popularized by Père Claude
Bernard (1588–1641). *A Book of Prayer* (Washington, DC: ICEL, 1987).

Salutation of St. Francis of Assisi

Holy Virgin Mary,
among women
there is no one like you born into the world:
you are the daughter
and the servant of the most high and supreme King
and Father of heaven,
you are the mother of our most holy Lord Jesus
Christ,
you are the spouse of the Holy Spirit.
Pray for us

with Saint Michael the Archangel
and all the powers of the heavens
and all the saints
to your most holy beloved Son, the Lord and Master.

Saint Francis of Assisi, O.F.M. (1181-1226), "The Office of the Passion",
trans. Regis J. Armstrong, O.F.M., Cap. and Ignatius Brady, O.F.M.

Acknowledgments

The publisher gratefully acknowledges the permission of the following copyright holders for the use of their texts in this book (publishers are listed alphabetically.)

Excerpts from St. Proclus, Sermon One on Mary, from The Documents of Early Christian Thought edited by Maurice Wiles and Mark Santer. Copyright © 1977 by Cambridge University Press. Reprinted with the permission of Cambridge University Press.

The icon "Virgin of the great sign" is used by permission of the Carmelites of Terre Haute, Indiana. Mounted icons and cards of various sizes are available from: Carmelite Monastery, 59 Allendale, Terre Haute, IN 47802 or call (812) 299-1410.

Excerpts from Homilies in Praise of the Blessed Virgin Mary. Copyright © 1993 by Cistercian Publications. Used with permission of the publisher.

Excerpted from Man, Monk, Mystic by Michael Casey, OCSO. Copyright © 1990 by Cistercian Publications. Used with permission of the publisher.

Excerpts *Praise God in Song* by William G. Storey and John A. Melloh. Copyright © 1982 by GIA Publications Inc., Chicago, IL. All rights reserved. Used with permission.

Canticle of Zachary by Carl P. Daw, Jr. © 1989 Hope Publishing Co., Carol Stream, IL 60188. All rights reserved. Used with permission.